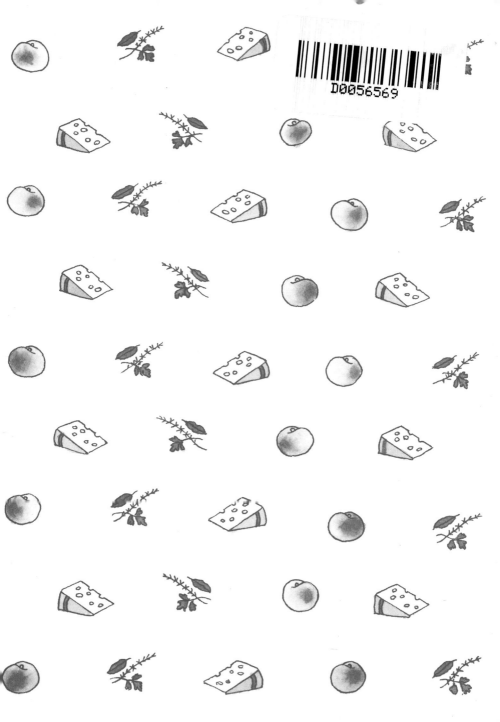

D0056569

FRENCH COOKING FOR BEGINNERS

Also by Helene Siegel

Italian Cooking for Beginners
Chinese Cooking for Beginners
Mexican Cooking for Beginners

COAUTHOR

Ma Cuisine Cooking School Cookbook
City Cuisine

THE ETHNIC KITCHEN

FRENCH COOKING FOR BEGINNERS

75 RECIPES FOR THE EAGER COOK

HELENE SIEGEL

ILLUSTRATIONS BY YAN NASCIMBENE

HarperCollins Publishers

HarperCollins books may be purchased for
educational, business, or sales promotional use. For
information please write: Special Markets
Department, HarperCollins Publishers, Inc.,
10 East 53rd Street, New York, NY 10022.

FIRST EDITION

Designed by Stephanie Tevonian

Library of Congress Cataloging-in-Publication Data
Siegel, Helene.
    French cooking for beginners : 75 recipes for
the eager cook / Helene Siegel.
        p.   cm.—(The ethnic kitchen)
    Includes index.
    ISBN 0-06-016431-X
    1. Cookery, French. I. Title. II. Series:
Siegel, Helene.
Ethnic kitchen.
TX719.S48   1994   93-30941
641.5944—dc20

94 95 96 97 98 DT/RRD 10 9 8 7 6 5 4 3 2

For Ted, simply the best

CONTENTS

Thanks to John Wainer for the first trip to France. And to Esther Davidowitz for the last.

HOW TO COOK FRENCH FOOD

EVERYDAY FRENCH cooking is no more complicated or costly than any other style of cooking. It is just more French—which means the bread should be fresh, the salad crisp, and the butter sweet.

FRENCH cooking means bringing an attitude of caring and respect as well as technique into the kitchen and the marketplace. At its best, it is cooking with the heart as well as the hands, and it needn't be haute to be so.

FRENCH cooking is as simple as roasted eggplant soup or browned onions heaped on top of a store-bought pizza shell and scattered with thyme and tiny Niçoise olives. It can be as light as a garden salad tossed with vinaigrette, as fast as seared tuna or salmon, as easy as roasted chicken, as earthy as lentil salad, or as robust as braised lamb shanks or mashed potatoes with garlic. If it is cooked with care and served with love, it is in the French style.

ALONG with the love may come a generous serving of cream, butter, eggs, and a certain amount of ceremony. Dairy products, traditionally associated with northern and central French cooking, round out flavors, thicken sauces, and in general create the more subtle or refined dishes associated with haute cuisine. Since I am as obsessed with my waistline as the next person, most of the recipes included here reflect the current preference for the lusty olive oil-based cooking of the south, and the rustic stews and easy casseroles that have come to be called "bistro" cooking.

WHEN butter and cream are called for, you can be sure that those ingredients were carefully measured out and judiciously applied. So when you do choose to indulge in a sensuous beurre blanc sauce

OR TREAT YOUR GUESTS TO A FABULOUS POTATO GRATIN, DON'T HAVE AN ANXIETY ATTACK. JUST RELAX AND REMEMBER THE FRENCH PARADOX. DRINK PLENTY OF RED WINE AND DIET TOMORROW.

AS FOR ALL THE CEREMONY SURROUNDING THE MEAL, FRENCH CHEFS AND MAÎTRE D'S HAVE BEEN SO SUCCESSFUL IN SETTING THE STANDARDS FOR THE REST OF THE WORLD, THEY HAVE MANAGED TO LEAVE A CLOUD OF CONFUSION AND INTIMIDATION IN THEIR WAKE. CENTRAL TO THE FRENCH AESTHETIC IS THE IDEA OF A PROGRESSION OF COURSES WHERE CONTRASTING TASTES, TEXTURES, AND TEMPERATURES CREATE A HARMONIOUS WHOLE. SINCE THE EYE SENDS A MESSAGE TO THE BRAIN FIRST, PRESENTATION ALWAYS MATTERS, ALTHOUGH IT NEED NOT NECESSARILY BE FANCY.

WHEN ENTERTAINING AT HOME, THESE PRINCIPLES CAN BE TRANSLATED TO A FEW SIMPLE MAXIMS: NEVER SERVE A CREAM SAUCE WITH A CREAM SAUCE; ALWAYS END A HEAVY MEAL WITH SOMETHING LIGHT, REFRESHING, AND PREFERABLY PRETTY; SEVERAL COURSES SERVED IN SMALLER PORTIONS MAKE FOR MORE INTERESTING MEALS; TABLE LINEN AND FLOWERS AID THE DIGESTION; AND WHITE PORCELAIN IS ALWAYS A SURE THING.

WHEN ALL IS SAID AND DONE, FOOD, ALONG WITH WINE, IS MEANT TO BE SAVORED SLOWLY AND ENJOYED WITH FRIENDS GRACIOUSLY—NOT WORRIED TO DEATH. TO THE FRENCH IT IS NATURAL TO CARE PASSIONATELY ABOUT WHAT THEY EAT AND HOW THEY EAT IT. IT IS A WAY OF LIFE.

FRENCH ASTRONAUT PATRICK BAUDRY, WHO TRAVELED INTO SPACE ABOARD THE AMERICAN SPACECRAFT *DISCOVERY* IN 1985 AND BROUGHT ALONG HIS OWN CRAB MOUSSE, ALSATIAN STEWED HARE, AND PÂTES DE FRUIT RATHER THAN PARTAKE OF THE CUISINE OF THE AMERICAN SPACE PROGRAM, PUT IT THIS WAY: "OUR FOOD TRADITION IS VERY ANCIENT. IT IS PART OF OUR CIVILIZATION. IT IS VERY IMPORTANT."

A FEW TECHNIQUES
FOR THE NOVICE

From soup to dessert, the language of the American or European kitchen is essentially French. Here is a small glossary of popular French cooking terms and some tips on how to translate them into action in your own kitchen.

TO SAUTÉ literally means "to jump," which is what your ingredients are supposed to do when the pan is hot enough. Always sauté quickly over high heat, with a minimum of fat, so the food changes color or browns. To avoid excess moisture in the pan, place the dry pan over high heat for a few seconds. Then add the fat and the food to be fried. Professionals and television chefs shake the pan for even browning and to avoid scorching—a technique that takes some practice. Frequent stirring will accomplish the same thing. The main pitfall for home cooks is sautéing in a pan that is too cool. Since chefs sauté with a higher flame than you can possibly attain on a home range, do not be afraid of pumping up the gas.

TO SWEAT, a professional cooking term inching its way into chefs' cookbooks, is almost the opposite of sautéing. Also done on the stovetop, it is slow cooking over low heat in a covered pan until the food is limp and does not change color. The resulting ingredients, often vegetables, develop a delicate flavor from steaming in their own juices.

TO REDUCE means to boil a liquid to concentrate its flavors by diminishing its volume. It is the most popular and least caloric way to thicken a sauce. Whenever instructions say to reduce, turn the heat to high and let the liquid boil rapidly. Refrain from stirring since that will lower the temperature in the pan and slow down the process. Unless a huge quantity is to be reduced, stay nearby and keep an eye on the pan. Judge the amount to be reduced by eye, by noticing its level on the sides of the pan or on a wooden spoon dipped in the liquid. It is not necessary to measure, as instructions are estimates, and the rhythm of this type of cooking is fast. Wine, vinegar, stock, and cream are the liquids most often reduced.

TO BLANCH means to cook very briefly in rapidly boiling water, just to soften slightly or loosen the skin. After draining, ingredients are either rinsed with cold water or plunged into an ice water bath to stop the cooking. I prefer blanching to steaming for lightly cooked vegetables be-

French Cooking for Beginners

cause it keeps their color bright. Tough vegetables like broccoli or carrots are often cooked in two steps, first blanched and then sautéed.

To DEGLAZE means to add liquid to a pan in which something has been sautéed in order to release the flavorful browned bits from the bottom and incorporate them into a sauce or gravy. First add the liquid, then raise the heat and use a wooden spoon to stir and scrape the bottom of the pan to release the browned bits.

To MAKE A MIREPOIX, chopped or finely diced onions, carrots, and celery are sweated or sautéed at the beginning of soups, stews, or braised meat dishes to add a subtle flavor to the broth. When these aromatics are chopped the mixture is called a mirepoix, when they are finely diced it is called brunoise.

To GET THE MOST FROM THE LEAST when cooking with butter or cream, use these rich products as supporting rather than featured players. The trick is to add them near the end of cooking time so their delicacy is still apparent. Instead of a beurre blanc, make a quick sauce by stirring a tablespoon or so of butter and some lemon juice and herbs into the pan juices after sautéing a piece of salmon or chicken; enrich a reduction from a stew by stirring in a tablespoon of butter before serving; or mellow out a puréed vegetable soup by finishing it with a spoonful of cream rather than giving it the full creamed soup treatment.

To THICKEN A SAUCE WITH EGG YOLKS, heat needs to be introduced slowly or the eggs will form curds rather than a thick, smooth coating. The key is to stir some of the hot cooking liquid into the yolks first, and then slowly incorporate that back into the hot mixture. (This step is called tempering.) Always cook over low heat once the eggs have been added, and stir constantly to keep the temperature low. Never bring egg-thickened sauces to a boil or the eggs will separate and scramble. Egg sauces are best served immediately.

To GRATINÉ a dish means to sprinkle the top with breadcrumbs or cheese and run the dish under the broiler so a crust forms. A gratin is both the name of a small baking dish and a finished dish of thinly sliced, layered vegetables usually baked in the oven and occasionally gratinéed.

HOW TO SHOP FOR FRENCH COOKING

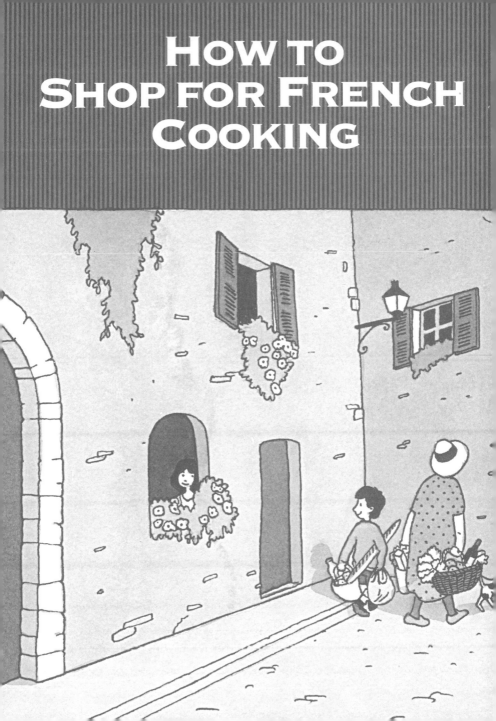

ALL BUT THE MOST LUXURIOUS FRENCH INGREDIENTS ARE STOCKED IN THE SUPERMARKET. BUT THE BEST WAY TO CAPTURE THE SPIRIT OF FRENCH CONNOISSEURSHIP IS TO EXPLORE LOCAL FARMERS' MARKETS AND SPECIALTY SHOPS AND DECIDE FOR YOURSELF WHO MAKES THE BEST BAGUETTE, WHOSE TOMATOES NOT ONLY LOOK GOOD BUT TASTE GOOD, WHERE TO FIND FRESH CHERVIL, AND WHICH BUTCHER IS KNOWLEDGEABLE AND HONEST ENOUGH TO DISCUSS THE BEST CUTS OF BEEF FOR A CASSOULET OR HOW TO COOK A POT ROAST PROPERLY. (FRENCH BUTCHERS ARE FAMOUS FOR THEIR RECIPES AS WELL AS THEIR WAY WITH A SHARP CLEAVER.) A WEEKLY VISIT TO A LOCAL FARMERS' MARKET, THE CLOSEST THING WE HAVE TO THE TRADITIONAL OPEN AIR MARKETS OF FRANCE, IS WONDERFUL FOR KEEPING IN TOUCH WITH SEASONAL PRODUCE AND VENDORS WHO CARE PASSIONATELY ABOUT THEIR WARES.

INGREDIENTS

Note: An asterisk preceding an ingredient indicates an item recommended for daily cooking.

The French repertoire is extremely flexible. Once you understand the basic cooking techniques, almost any ingredient can be incorporated to give traditional dishes a new twist. I have tasted an excellent tuna with beurre blanc sauce seasoned with Chinese black beans, and an egg-thickened sauce for chicken brought to life with cumin and cilantro. These, then, are the basic products that make all those other ingredients taste French.

GRAINS

*BREAD is as essential to the French diet as red wine and coffee. It is bought fresh every day and served at every meal. Leftover bread may be used for breadcrumbs or croutons; the thrifty French *never* throw it out.

The two French breads widely available here are long thin crusty baguettes and the doughier large round crusty loaves known as pain de campagne or country bread, made with white or wheat flour. Both are wonderful all-purpose breads for accompanying meals. Country breads last a little longer and baguettes are better for making croutons. Shop around until you find the best source in your neighborhood and avoid most of the so-called French bread baked in supermarket bakeries. It doesn't come close to the real crusty, chewy thing. In France, where its price is regulated by the government, bread is rarely if ever baked at home and never served with butter.

DRY BREAD CRUMBS are easy to make from stale baguettes. If the bread is not totally dry, trim the crusts and place in a 300 F oven for 15 to 30 minutes. Then cut into cubes and grind in a food processor until fine. Store in plastic bags or containers at room temperature up to 2 weeks, or in the freezer up to 3 months. Bread crumbs need not be defrosted before using.

CROUTONS, or toasted bread for garnishing soups and serving with pâtés and spreads, are similar to Italian bruschetta. Thinly slice a baguette, spread the slices on a baking sheet, and toast in a 400 F oven until golden brown, about 7 minutes per side. Drizzle with olive oil or melted butter as desired. For toasted cubes, cut bread into cubes first and then sauté in oil in a hot skillet.

*Egg Noodles are a good accompaniment to many of the stewed or braised dishes popular in the country kitchen. Dishes like boeuf bourguignon, blanquette de veau, and lamb shanks benefit from the soothing starchiness of a bed of wide egg noodles. Simply boil, drain, and toss with a little butter before topping with the preceding foods.

Couscous resembles a small yellow grain, though it is classified as a pasta since it is made of semolina and water. It is a popular starch accompaniment in France, especially for brochettes and stews, and is also the name of the Moroccan dish consisting of the grains topped with a spicy stew of chicken or lamb. Precooked couscous is available in speciality shops and the international section of some supermarkets and can be reconstituted by combining the grains with an equal amount of boiling water or stock or by following the package directions. Untreated couscous, which is much more time-consuming to cook, is difficult to find in American markets and demands a special utensil called a couscoussière for steaming.

Long-grain white rice is also an excellent accompaniment to traditional French foods.

French Cooking for Beginners

OILS AND VINEGARS

*OLIVE OIL is used in southern France, as it is in Italy, for sautéing, dressing salads, and making uncooked sauces like mayonnaise. Although French extra virgin olive oil is exported, it is relatively expensive and difficult to find. I recommend using Italian olive oil—pure for cooking and extra virgin for dressing—for Mediterranean-style dishes. For most other cooking a fairly tasteless oil like *vegetable* or *safflower* oil is fine. Rare oils such as walnut and hazelnut oil should be reserved for salads and are not a necessity in the home pantry. Always store oil in a cool, dark place.

*RED WINE VINEGAR AND WHITE WINE VINEGAR are used for dressing salads, deglazing pans, and reducing sauces. There is very little difference in taste, although white vinegar is preferable in pale sauces because of its lack of color. Large bottles of French wine vinegar, available at specialty shops, are inexpensive and can be stored indefinitely in a cool, dark place. Once again, specialty vinegars such as raspberry or tarragon are not necessary for daily cooking. You can flavor your own vinegars by adding a sprig or two of your favorite fresh herb to a bottle of vinegar and letting it steep for about 2 weeks.

DAIRY

*UNSALTED OR SWEET BUTTER is de rigueur for French cooking and baking. Do not substitute margarine (which, by the way, was invented by the French), especially for sauce-making, as it will not behave properly. Professionals always prefer unsalted butter for cooking because they can better control the finished flavor. Sweet butter also tends to be fresher, since salt is a preservative. French butter, available at some specialty shops, is made with less water and has a silkier consistency and sweeter flavor than American butter.

MILK. In French recipes calling for milk, use whole rather than reduced fat milk, since it has the body and richness called for in such foods as ice cream, custards, and gratins.

HEAVY OR WHIPPING CREAM is as basic to provincial cooking as it is to haute cuisine. It adds a characteristic richness to sauces and desserts without which they wouldn't be French. American heavy cream has an exceptionally long shelf life; it will keep in the refrigerator about a month. Do not substitute sour cream or yogurt in cooked dishes, as they will separate if brought to a boil. If you must save some calories, use half and half instead.

CRÈME FRAÎCHE is a French cream with a high butterfat content and slightly fermented flavor. It can be purchased at cheese and specialty shops or you can make it at home: Combine 1 cup heavy cream with 2 tablespoons buttermilk. Cover and let sit at room temperature about 24 hours to thicken and then store in the refrigerator up to 1 week. Heavy cream may always be substituted.

*EGGS are used regularly in the French kitchen to enrich and thicken sauces and to lighten and add volume to desserts and baked goods. As chef Paul Bocuse so bluntly told author Calvin Trillin, "Without butter, without eggs, there is no reason to come to France." The recipes in this book were tested with eggs graded "large" unless otherwise specified in ingredients lists. Since beginners may be put off at the prospect of separating eggs, here's the skinny: Eggs are easier to separate when cold, although whites can be whipped to greater height at room temperature. Working over a bowl to catch the whites, crack the eggs on the side of the bowl or counter. Using half of the shell to catch the yolk, gently pour out the white, being careful not to let any yolk get in it, and then let the yolks slide into another bowl. Fingers are also good separators; just let the whites slip through partially opened fingers. If yolk does get in the whites, remove it with an egg shell or discard and start over again, since whites will not rise with yolk or any other grease in them.

CHEESE is more often eaten at the end of the meal than used as an ingredient in France. The most popular cheeses for cooking are Gruyère and Parmesan. When adding cheese to a sauce, always crumble it first, apply minimum heat just to melt, and remove before it turns grainy.

CONDIMENTS

*GARLIC is king in Provence, where it is a main ingredient in dishes like chicken with forty cloves, and aioli. It fades away to a whisper in other regions, especially the dairy regions of the north. In the southern port city of Marseilles, there is a wonderful outdoor market devoted entirely to garlic, where you can choose among thick braids of white, violet, or rose garlic heads from competing farmers. White is the mildest and rose the strongest, with violet somewhere in between. Your local farmers' market may also stock different types. Purchase hard heads of garlic and store in a cool, dry place. If you find a green sprout in the center of a clove, remove it before chopping.

OLIVES, one of the oldest known fruits, are eaten as a snack and used as an ingredient in spreads, sauces, and stuffings in southern France.

Small black Niçoise and green picholine, easily found here, are good for salads and nibbling, and the larger Greek Kalamata and green French country olives for cooking. Olives should always be stored in their brine or oil in the refrigerator.

CAPERS, the pickled buds of a bush that grows wild along the Mediterranean, are an essential flavoring in Provençal cooking, where they are used on pizzas, in spreads like tapenade (which means caper in Provençal), and in sauces. The best are the small nonpareil type, available in bottles at the supermarket. They may be stored in their brine in the refrigerator indefinitely.

ANCHOVIES are used liberally in southern French cooking. They are a main ingredient in the pungent spread anchoiade and indispensable to Niçoise salads and pizzas. Spanish anchovies, packed in salt and oil and sold in small resealable jars, are much more convenient for storing than tins. Once opened, they keep in the refrigerator indefinitely.

*MUSTARD, the most popular condiment in France, is used to flavor sauces and salad dressings including classic vinaigrette and mayonnaise. It has been made in Dijon, the capital of Burgundy, since the fourteenth century. Although it now comes from just about anywhere, if it is smooth, pale yellow, and made of mustard seeds ground with white wine vinegar, salt, and water, it is still considered Dijon—the best type for cooking. When cooking with mustard, always apply at the last moment and remove from heat, since it loses its flavor quickly. Good brands from France are available at the supermarket. Once opened, mustard should always be stored in the refrigerator.

SALT PORK is unsmoked slab bacon from the belly of the pig. It is traditionally cut into lardons or small chunks for flavoring stews like coq au vin and boeuf bourguignon, tossing in salads, and enriching meats for roasting. Wrap leftover salt pork well and store in the freezer up to 6 months. It defrosts quickly. Slab or thickly sliced bacon can be substituted, though to be authentic it should first be blanched for 2 or 3 minutes to remove the smokiness. I find bacon preferable, because of its higher percentage of meat to fat, for salads. Always cook salt pork over low heat to avoid toughening. Salt pork is available at the supermarket next to the bacon.

*CHOCOLATE, which came to France from the New World primarily as a drink, is a favorite ingredient for baking and dessert-making in France. Purchase good quality semi or bittersweet chocolate in bulk and store, well wrapped in a cool, dry place. Do not worry if it develops a "bloom," or white powder on the surface. This is caused by warm temperatures, which make the cocoa butter rise. The chocolate is fine; it keeps a good long time. You will be amazed at the difference a quality brand makes in chocolate desserts.

VEGETABLES AND FRUITS

France is the richest agricultural region of Europe. Artichokes, eggplant, fennel, tomatoes, peppers, green beans, and zucchini abound in the south; mushrooms, peas, asparagus, and leeks reign in the center; onions, parsnips, beets, cabbage, and turnips turn up in the north; and potatoes are king everywhere. As for fruit, the most popular for baking are apples, pears, apricots, and, of course, berries—with lemons kept on hand for seasoning sauces and whipping up wonderful lemon curd tarts.

ONIONS. In the French kitchen careful distinctions are made about each member of the onion family:

*YELLOW ONIONS are used as aromatics, often in combination with carrots and celery, to flavor soups, stews, and braised dishes. They are also a main ingredient in dishes like onion soup and pissaladière, or onion pizza. Store in a cool, dark place—not the refrigerator.

*SHALLOTS are small purple brown-skinned onions with a strong, concentrated flavor. They are used mostly in sauces, where they are often reduced with wine or vinegar before the sauce is thickened. Shallots, like onions, are always peeled before using. Each bulb contains a few layered cloves, each considered a shallot. Store as you would onions.

LEEKS, known as "poor man's asparagus" in France, enjoy a special place in soups, stews, tarts, and gratins. They have a milder, sweeter flavor than other onions and don't cause the eyes to tear when cut. To clean, first trim and discard the roots and green stalks. Cut in half lengthwise and rinse under cold, running water, separating the layers with your fingers to remove any dirt. Store in the vegetable bin of the refrigerator.

PEARL OR BABY ONIONS are the tiny white onions, not to be confused with boiling onions, that are used as a garnish for dishes cooked Burgundy style such as coq au vin. They help reduce the richness of the sauce. To prepare as a garnish, trim the ends and blanch in boiling water. Rinse with cold water and then squeeze to remove the skins. Store delicate pearl onions in the refrigerator for only a few days.

WINE AND SPIRITS

These are used without fanfare in the French kitchen. The general rule when cooking with wine is to use an inexpensive wine you consider good enough for everyday drinking, such as vin ordinaire in France. Once wine is cooked, the alcohol evaporates and the flavor becomes more concentrated, so a wine that has gone bad or was never very good to begin with will only worsen. I keep on hand a couple of moderately priced bottles of dry white wine like Chardonnay or Sauvignon Blanc and a full-flavored red wine like Cabernet Sauvignon for cooking. Opened bottles can be recorked and stored in the refrigerator about a week. Always taste before using.

*BRANDY is the most frequently used spirit for flambés, sauces, and desserts. Although imported Cognac and Armagnac are considered the best, I find California brandy good enough for cooking. I also recommend keeping a small bottle of either apple or pear brandy in the pantry for pastries and fruit accompaniments. They can be used interchangeably in emergencies.

LIQUEURS are generally used to finish sauces or flavor rich custards and desserts. As such, they are rarely boiled down. My two favorites for French cooking are anise-flavored Pernod for Mediterranean foods and orange-flavored Grand Marnier for desserts. Other orange liqueurs such as triple sec or Cointreau are also fine.

HERBS

Herbs are used subtly in the French kitchen to highlight rather than overwhelm other flavors. Fresh is preferable to dry whenever possible. When you do substitute dry, use about one-third the quantity and add the dried herbs at the beginning to reconstitute their flavor. Fresh herbs, except for an occasional sprig of rosemary or thyme, are usually cooked briefly toward the end of cooking just to release their flavor. Often it is better to substitute another fresh herb rather than the dried one.

FINES HERBES, a subtle combination of chopped fresh parsley, chervil, chives, and tarragon, is used to flavor omelettes, and occasionally grilled fish and chicken.

HERBES DE PROVENCE is a combination of dried herbs that may include thyme, oregano, marjoram, chervil, rosemary, bay leaves, and summer savory. If you already stock most of the herbs you can just mix your own combination when a recipe asks for it—unless you just have to own the earthenware crock in which it is commercially available.

*THYME, which originated in the Mediterranean region of France, suggests French cooking the way basil does Italian. Its tiny green leaf and subtle fragrance enhance meat, poultry, vegetables, fish, and even fruits like lemon, prune, and apple. It goes into the classic bouquet garni for stock-making, and dries well. Substitute the dried herb or a smaller quantity of fresh chopped oregano.

TARRAGON has a slender, long, dark green leaf and a strong licorice flavor. It is the primary flavoring in béarnaise sauce and goes well with chicken, fish, shellfish, eggs, and tomatoes. Try to find the fresh herb, as the dried one doesn't have much flavor. Fresh basil is a suitable substitute.

CHERVIL has a thin stem, a bright green lacy leaf, and a mild anise flavor. Since it is so delicate, it can be used either whole or lightly chopped, as a garnish for soups, salads, eggs, and tomato dishes. Chervil is difficult to find at the supermarket and is not available dried. Italian parsley is a good substitute.

CHIVES, with their simple shape, bright green color, and slight onion flavor, are a wonderful garnish for eggs, fish, soups, and salads. They are not often cooked. Either eliminate or substitute another herb, but do not use dried chives as a garnish.

*ITALIAN PARSLEY, with its thinner texture and subtler flavor, is preferable to the curly variety. Parsley, including the stems, is required for making stocks and soups and as a garnish. The dried herb may be used for lengthily cooked foods, or substitute curly parsley.

*BAY LEAVES are used sparingly in soups, marinades, pickles, and stews. A leaf is always included in a bouquet garni.

ROSEMARY, BASIL, AND SAGE are used primarily in Provençal cooking.

BOUQUET GARNI is a bundle of herbs and spices enclosed in a cheesecloth sack for easy removal from soups, stews, and stocks. The content varies according to what is being cooked, but a typical bouquet garni contains a subtle combination of parsley, thyme, bay leaves, and black peppercorns. If you don't stock kitchen string, you can gather the four corners of cheesecloth and tie them together to seal the packet. If you don't stock cheesecloth, you can stuff the herbs in the hollow of a small celery rib topped by another and then tied together. Of course, if you don't have string or cheesecloth and are feeling rebellious, you can always just add the ingredients to the pot and strain them out at the end. I promise not to tell.

EQUIPMENT FOR THE FRENCH KITCHEN

If there is one thing I've learned from observing cooking teachers and chefs, it is that good equipment does make a difference both in the finished product and the effort it takes to produce it. Although the French kitchen does not call for anything special, here are the bare essentials for producing French food with the requisite joie de vivre.

High quality *knives* are well worth the investment. All you need is a 3- or 4-inch paring knife for small jobs, an 8-inch chef's knife for most chopping and slicing, and a medium serrated blade for bread, tomatoes, and citrus fruits. Purchase the best you can afford, keep them sharp, store them well and they should last a lifetime. If you need a *cutting board*, the white plastic kind is preferable to wood since it can't warp or split. A wooden board is preferable for kneading bread and rolling pastry.

As for *pots and pans*, once again less in best. All you really need are two heavy saucepans—small and medium-sized—and a large stainless

pot for stocks and soups. For sautéing and sauce-making I recommend a good quality combination stainless and copper 10-inch skillet with oven-proof handle, and an 8-inch cast iron pan for omelettes and smaller quantities. An enameled cast-iron dutch oven is perfect for stews and braised dishes, and one or two large Pyrex roasting pans can be used for most roasts and casseroles. Tart pans with removable bottoms are a wonder for beautiful tarts and quiches.

Among *small gadgets*, some wooden spoons, rubber and metal spatulas, small and large ladles, mixing bowls, measuring cups and spoons, a good whisk, tongs, and a strainer are key for pulling everything together. And there are also two electrical appliances that will vastly improve your life—or at least your cooking.

The first is the *food processor*, which deserves at least as much credit as Julia Child for making French or "gourmet" cooking accessible. It can purée soups and sauces, grind nuts, grate cheese, combine a pâté or mousse, cut french fries, emulsify a hollandaise, and whip up a flaky tart dough or rugged country bread in minutes. The other appliance, for those who plan on baking or whipping up cream or many egg whites, is an *electric mixer*. If you are not ready for the commitment of a heavy-duty countertop model, you owe it to yourself to acquire a small hand-held electric model. Nothing takes the fun out of cooking and baking as quickly as aching arms and shoulders.

SOUPS, SALADS, AND APPETIZERS

MOST OF THESE STARTERS ARE FULL-FLAVORED AND SATISFYING ENOUGH TO MAKE WONDERFUL LITTLE MEALS ON THEIR OWN WITH SOME CRUSTY BREAD AND PERHAPS A GREEN SALAD. OTHER IDEAS FOR BEGINNING THE MEAL ARE THE ASPARAGUS QUICHE (PAGE 39), A HOT OR COLD RATATOUILLE (PAGE 84) WITH GRILLED BREAD, LENTIL SALAD (PAGE 85), OR ROASTED GARLIC (PAGE 80) SPREAD ON CROUTONS. AND IF YOU NEED A LITTLE SOMETHING EXTRA FOR NIBBLING BEFORE THE MEAL BEGINS THERE ARE ALWAYS THOSE CLASSIC FRENCH STANDBYS: A SELECTION OF PÂTÉS WITH OLIVES AND CORNICHONS, OR SMOKED SALMON OR CAVIAR ON THINLY SLICED, BUTTERED BREAD.

ROASTED
EGGPLANT SOUP

Roasted eggplant provides a depth of flavor sometimes lacking in low-calorie foods. This version was inspired by Champagne restaurant in Los Angeles, where it appears on the spa menu. *✕ Serves 4*

1 large eggplant
Olive oil
Salt
Freshly ground black pepper
1 onion, peeled and thinly sliced
4 garlic cloves, peeled and minced
¼ teaspoon ground cumin

1 quart homemade chicken stock,
   or 2 cups canned broth and
   2 cups water
3 tablespoons chopped fresh basil
¼ cup soft unripened goat cheese
   (optional)

1] Preheat the oven to 450 F.

2] Trim the eggplant, cut in half lengthwise, and score cut sides several times. Rub all over with olive oil, sprinkle with salt and pepper, and place on a baking sheet, cut sides up. Bake until the flesh feels soft when pressed with a finger, about 1 hour. Set aside to cool.

3] When cool enough to handle, peel and discard the eggplant's skin. Place the flesh in a food processor fitted with the metal blade, or in a blender, and purée until smooth.

4] Heat 2 tablespoons olive oil in a large dutch oven or stockpot over medium-low heat. Cook the onion, garlic, 1 teaspoon salt, ½ teaspoon black pepper, and cumin until the onion is soft, about 10 minutes. Stir in the puréed eggplant and chicken stock. Bring to a boil, reduce to a simmer, and skim the foam that rises to the top. Cook, uncovered, 10 minutes.

5] Transfer to a food processor or blender and purée until smooth. (To avoid spills, if using a food processor, pulse several times before puréeing. If using a blender, purée in batches.) Pour back into the soup pot, sprinkle with basil, and simmer 5 minutes more. Remove from heat, stir in crumbled goat cheese if desired, and serve hot.

PISTOU

This thick, rich Provençal vegetable soup made with a pesto (pistou) base is similar to an Italian minestrone. If you don't have time to make fresh pesto for it, substitute store-bought pesto, or just toss in a handful of freshly grated Parmesan and some chopped basil before serving.
✖ *Serves 6*

2 medium red potatoes, with skins
2 carrots, peeled
3 leeks, white part only, cut in half lengthwise and washed
2 zucchinis, ends trimmed
1 yellow crookneck squash, ends trimmed
One 15-ounce can white kidney beans or cannellini beans
2 large tomatoes, peeled, seeded, and diced
¼ pound green beans, trimmed and cut in ½-inch lengths
8 cups chicken broth
½ teaspoon salt
Freshly ground black pepper
Pesto (recipe follows)

1] Finely dice the potatoes, carrots, leeks, zucchinis, and squash. Place the white beans in a strainer to drain, and rinse under cold water to remove canning liquid. Place the potatoes, carrots, and leeks in one bowl and the remaining vegetables with beans and tomatoes in another bowl for bringing to the stove.

2] Pour the chicken broth into a stockpot or large dutch oven and bring to a boil. With a ladle, skim and discard any foam that rises to the top. Add the potatoes, carrots, and leeks, reduce to a simmer, and cook, uncovered, 15 minutes. Add the remaining vegetables and beans. Bring the stock back to a boil and reduce to simmer. Cook, uncovered, about 15 minutes longer, or until the green beans are done to your taste. Add the salt and pepper, being careful not to oversalt, since the pesto is salty.

3] To serve, place a generous dollop of pesto in each serving bowl. Ladle in the soup and bring to the table with remaining pesto to add to taste.

PESTO

2 cups basil leaves
3 garlic cloves, peeled
$\frac{1}{2}$ cup olive oil

$\frac{1}{2}$ teaspoon coarse salt
$\frac{1}{2}$ cup plus 2 tablespoons grated
  Parmesan cheese

1] In a food processor fitted with the metal blade, or in a blender, combine basil, garlic, olive oil, and salt. Process until a smooth paste is formed.

2] Scrape down the sides of the bowl once or twice to avoid large chunks of garlic. Add the cheese and pulse to combine.

3] Set aside or refrigerate if making in advance. Pesto may be stored in the refrigerator with a thin layer of olive oil on top for a month or so.

FRENCH ONION SOUP

French onion soup, with its crusty crouton and crown of melted cheese, has always found an appreciative audience this side of the Atlantic. It makes a nice winter lunch with a green salad and a glass of red wine. ✕ *Serves 4*

4 tablespoons (½ stick) unsalted butter
4 yellow onions, about 2½ pounds, peeled and thinly sliced across the width
2 teaspoons salt
1 teaspoon sugar
1 teaspoon white pepper
2 tablespoons all-purpose flour

Two 14½-ounce cans beef broth, or 4 cups stock
Eight ¼-inch slices French bread or baguette
½ pound Gruyère or Swiss cheese, half cut into 8 slices and half grated
1 tablespoon port (optional)

1] Melt the butter in a large stockpot over medium heat. Add the sliced onions, salt, sugar, and pepper. Cook, stirring frequently, until the onions begin to brown, about 40 minutes. Occasionally scrape and stir the bottom of the pan to incorporate the browned bits that add flavor.

2] Sprinkle in the flour, stirring constantly, until the flour is golden, or cooked. Then slowly pour in the beef broth and 1½ cups water, stirring constantly to avoid lumping. When all the liquid has been added, bring to a low boil and simmer, uncovered, 10 minutes.

3] Meanwhile preheat the broiler.

4] Spread the baguette slices on a baking tray and place under the broiler until golden on one side, about a minute. Remove from broiler, turn the bread over, and cover each bread slice with a slice of cheese. Return to the broiler, just long enough to melt the cheese, about a minute. Transfer 2 bread slices to the bottom of each soup bowl.

5] As the soup is finishing, stir in the port, if desired, and taste and adjust the seasonings. Ladle into the prepared soup bowls and bring to the table with remaining grated cheese.

COLD TOMATO AND CUCUMBER SOUP

A wonderful choice for summer entertaining, this elegant cold tomato soup is like a smooth, simplified gazpacho. It should be well chilled—a day in the refrigerator is fine—and served with croutons or toasted bread. Use the best ripe tomatoes you can find for such a briefly cooked, clean-tasting soup. ✖ *Serves 4*

2½ pounds ripe tomatoes
2 tablespoons olive oil
2 garlic cloves, peeled and roughly chopped
½ teaspoon salt
Freshly ground black pepper
2 large cucumbers, peeled, seeded, and roughly chopped

½ cup tomato juice, or more as needed
1½ tablespoons red wine vinegar
3 dashes Tabasco
2 tablespoons thinly sliced fresh chives for garnish

1] Trim the stems and cut an X in the bottom of each tomato for easy peeling. Bring water to a boil in a medium saucepan and submerge tomatoes for 20 seconds. With a slotted spoon transfer tomatoes to a bowl of cold water to stop the cooking. Peel and cut each tomato in half across the width. Working over the sink, gently squeeze to remove and discard seeds. Roughly chop the tomatoes.

2] Heat the olive oil in a medium skillet over moderate heat. Briefly cook the garlic just to release its aroma, about 2 minutes, then add the tomatoes, salt, and pepper. Cook at a moderate boil, stirring occasionally, for 5 minutes. Remove from heat.

3] Place the cucumbers in a food processor fitted with the metal blade, or in a blender, and purée. Add the tomatoes and the remaining ingredients. Continue puréeing until smooth. (If your tomatoes are not quite ripe, or too dry, you may need to add extra tomato juice to compensate.) Transfer to a container to chill until serving time, at least 8 hours. Ladle into serving bowls and sprinkle chives across the top.

SALADE LYONNAISE

Here the classic salad of bitter greens, hot bacon, and warm vinaigrette called *pissenlits* takes on an extra dollop of flavor from poached egg. ✖ *Serves 4*

1 large head curly endive, frisée, escarole, or dandelion greens, about 4 cups
¼ pound thickly sliced bacon, cut across the width in ¼-inch strips
¼ cup white wine vinegar
4 eggs

¼ cup red wine vinegar
1 tablespoon safflower or vegetable oil
Salt and freshly ground black pepper
1½ tablespoons sliced fresh chives

1] Wash and thoroughly dry the lettuce. Break into bite-sized pieces and place in a mixing bowl in the refrigerator.

2] Fry the bacon in a skillet over moderate heat, stirring and tossing with a slotted spoon, until crisp. Then transfer to paper towels to drain and reserve the drippings in the pan.

3] While the bacon is frying, fill a large skillet nearly to the rim with water for poaching the eggs. Add the white wine vinegar and bring to a simmer. Crack each egg, as close as possible to the water's surface, and gently slip it into the simmering water. Cook until the whites are just set and the yellows remain runny, 3 minutes for refrigerated eggs. Use a slotted spoon to transfer the eggs to a small bowl.

4] Pour the red wine vinegar, safflower oil, reserved bacon drippings, and fried bacon bits over the lettuce. Toss well and season with salt and pepper. Divide the salad into 4 serving bowls. Top each with an egg, sprinkle with chives and additional ground pepper on the egg, and serve warm with toasted bread.

WARM FIG AND CHÈVRE SALAD

In the late summer or early autumn look for soft, fragrant black or green figs with slightly cracked skins for mixing with greens and goat cheese in this sensual Riviera salad. ✕ *Serves 6*

12 cups or ¾ pound mixed baby lettuces such as arugula, mâche, radicchio, and frisée
3 tablespoons red wine vinegar
2 tablespoons lemon juice
1 tablespoon plus 1 teaspoon honey
½ cup mild olive oil, plus some for the figs and cheese

Salt and freshly ground black pepper
6 ripe black figs, stems removed, cut in half lengthwise
6 ounces soft unripened goat cheese log, cut into 12 slices across the width

1] Preheat the broiler.

2] Wash and thoroughly dry the lettuces; break into bite-sized pieces. Place in a large mixing bowl.

3] In a small bowl, whisk together the red wine vinegar, lemon juice, honey, and olive oil. Season to taste with salt and pepper. Pour over the salad greens and toss well to coat evenly. Divide into 6 portions and place in individual bowls.

4] Arrange the figs, cut side up, on a baking tray and top each with a slice of cheese. Lightly drizzle with olive oil. Place under the broiler until the cheese begins to brown and melt, about 3 minutes. Place 2 fig halves on top of each salad and serve.

PISSALADIÈRE

Pissaladière, or caramelized onion pizza, is sold by bakeries and pizzerias in southern France to be eaten out of hand as a snack or small lunch. This adaptation, made with prebaked Boboli crust, does not forfeit an ounce of flavor for ease of preparation. Cut into small wedges or squares for a buffet or serve larger wedges with a green salad for a satisfying weeknight supper. ✗ *Serves 6 as an appetizer*

2 pounds (about 4 medium) onions
¼ cup olive oil, plus extra for
   drizzling
1½ teaspoons salt
2 teaspoons fresh chopped thyme,
   or 1 teaspoon dried

Freshly ground black pepper
One 1-pound family-size Boboli
   pizza crust
8 anchovies, or 16 strips sun-dried
   tomatoes, packed in oil
¼ cup black Niçoise olives

1] Peel the onions and slice thinly across the width by hand or in a food processor fitted with the 4-mm blade.

2] In a large sauté pan, heat the olive oil over medium-low heat. Add the onions, salt, thyme, and pepper. Cover and cook until the onions are wilted and beginning to brown, about 40 minutes. Stir the onions occasionally, scraping up and mixing in any browned bits from the bottom of the pan—these caramelized bits add flavor.

3] Preheat the oven to 450 F.

4] Place the pizza crust on a baking tray. Spread the onion mixture over the crust, leaving the edges bare like a pizza. Arrange the anchovies or sun-dried tomatoes in a spoke pattern and sprinkle on the olives. Lightly drizzle with olive oil. Bake 10 minutes, or until the crust is crisp. Cut into wedges and serve warm or at room temperature.

EGGPLANT CAVIAR

I first tasted this lusty spread in the Marais, Paris's Jewish quarter, where it was served in a large crock with raw and pickled vegetables, delectable olives, and thinly sliced toasted baguettes. I immediately fell in love. It makes an excellent lunch, spread on some bread and topped, in summer, with sliced tomato. ✕ *Makes 2 cups, enough for 6 appetizer portions*

2 medium eggplants, ends trimmed
Pure olive oil
Salt
Freshly ground black pepper
4 garlic cloves, peeled
2 tablespoons extra virgin olive oil

3 tablespoons lemon juice
½ teaspoon cumin
½ medium onion, peeled and chopped
Strong black olives, raw vegetables, and toasted baguettes for garnish

1] Preheat oven to 450 F.

2] Cut the eggplants in half lengthwise and score each flat side with a few diagonal intersecting cuts. Lightly rub all over with pure olive oil and season with salt and pepper. Place on a baking tray, cut sides up. Bake until soft and partially blackened, about 1 hour. Set aside to cool.

3] Scrape the pulp out of the eggplants with a spoon, discarding the skins. To mince the garlic, drop the cloves down the tube of a food processor fitted with the metal blade while the machine is running. Remove lid and add the eggplant, extra virgin olive oil, lemon juice, ½ teaspoon salt, and some black pepper. Purée until smooth and light, about 2 minutes. Transfer to a bowl and gently stir in the diced onions. Serve, or chill until serving time. Eggplant caviar may be kept in the refrigerator up to 5 days.

CRUDITÉS WITH MEDITERRANEAN DIPS

━━━━━━━━━━━━━━■━━━━━━━━━━━━━

Here are a few robust dips for serving with raw vegetables, hard-boiled eggs, thinly sliced toasted baguettes, or crackers—and the best olives you can find.

ROASTED RED PEPPER SPREAD

✸ *Makes 2 cups*

4 red bell peppers
3 garlic cloves, peeled and minced
½ cup roughly chopped sun-dried tomatoes, packed in oil

3 tablespoons capers
2 tablespoons extra virgin olive oil
4 teaspoons red wine vinegar

1] Roast the peppers over a gas flame or under an electric broiler until they are charred all over. Transfer to a plastic bag to sweat for 10 minutes. Remove the stems, ribs, and seeds, peel, and cut the pulp into large pieces.

2] Place pieces in the bowl of a food processor fitted with the metal blade. Add the remaining ingredients and pulse about 5 times until a chunky spread is formed.

AIOLI

✗ Makes 2 cups

8 garlic cloves, peeled
2 egg yolks
Juice of 1 lemon

1 cup olive oil
½ cup safflower oil
Salt and black pepper

1] With the machine on, drop the garlic cloves down the tube of a food processor fitted with the metal blade. Process until minced.

2] Remove the lid and add the egg yolks and lemon juice. Process until smooth. With the machine running, pour in the oils in a slow steady stream. (If your machine comes with a plastic cylinder with a tiny hole in the center that fits in the feed tube, it will perfectly control the flow of oil.)

3] Season to taste with salt and pepper and process briefly just to combine. Aioli and other mayonnaise may be stored in the refrigerator up to 1 week. Do not freeze.

TUNA TAPENADE

✗ Makes 1 cup

1 garlic clove, peeled
One 6-ounce can imported tuna in
    olive oil
3 large, garlicky green olives, sliced
    off the pit

2 tablespoons lemon juice
2 tablespoons olive oil
Leaves only from 3 thyme sprigs
Freshly ground black pepper

1] With the machine on, drop the garlic clove down the tube of a food processor fitted with the metal blade and mince.

2] Add the tuna with its oil, olives, lemon juice, olive oil, thyme, and 3 or 4 grindings of fresh black pepper. Pulse until a chunky spread is formed.

MICHELE'S CHICKEN
LIVER MOUSSE

Good friend and hiking partner Michele Fuetsch serves this sumptuous chicken liver mousse at her annual Christmas party, after which at least three friends call her to ask for the recipe. An added bonus —the recipe, adapted from Diane Rossen Worthington's *The Cuisine of California,* also freezes well. ✕ *Makes 3¹/₂ cups, enough for 12 as an appetizer*

1 cup pine nuts
3 tablespoons unsalted butter
2 tablespoons vegetable oil
1 onion, peeled and chopped
2 shallots, peeled and chopped
1 pear, peeled, cored, and chopped
1 garlic clove, peeled and minced
12 ounces cream cheese (not whipped), cut in cubes

¹/₂ pound loose pork sausage
¹/₂ pound chicken livers, trimmed
¹/₄ cup pear liqueur
1 tablespoon chopped fresh thyme
¹/₄ teaspoon allspice
1¹/₂ teaspoons salt
2 tablespoons chopped fresh rosemary
¹/₂ teaspoon ground white pepper

1] Preheat the oven to 350 F. Spread the nuts on a baking sheet and toast in the oven until pale brown, about 8 minutes. Set aside.

2] In a medium skillet, heat the butter and 1 tablespoon of the oil over moderate heat. Cook the onion, shallots, and pear until soft, about 10 minutes. Add the garlic and cook another minute.

3] Transfer to a food processor fitted with the metal blade, add the cubed cream cheese, and purée until smooth. Reserve mixture in the food processor.

4] Heat the remaining tablespoon of oil in the same skillet over medium-high heat and sauté the pork and livers until the livers are barely pink in the center. (Test by cutting one open.) Carefully drain off excess fat and off the heat pour in the pear liqueur. Return to heat, light a match, and hold it close to the pan's surface to flame. When the flames subside, remove from the heat.

5] Transfer contents of skillet to the pear and onion mixture in the food processor and process briefly. Then add the remaining herbs and seasonings and process until smooth. Add the toasted pine nuts and process until smooth. Taste and adjust seasonings with salt and pepper.

French Cooking for Beginners

6] Spoon into a ceramic crock or terrine, smooth the surface, and chill at least 2 hours to marry the flavors before serving in the crock accompanied by thinly sliced baguette, crackers, or toast points.

MUSHROOMS
À LA GRECQUE

The technique for this classic hors d'oeuvre is really easy, although the ingredient list is long. The same formula can be applied to carrot or fennel strips. ✖ *Serves 4*

1 pound white mushrooms, trimmed and wiped clean
1 cup dry white wine
¼ cup white wine vinegar
1 large shallot, peeled and chopped
4 garlic cloves, peeled and crushed
1 teaspoon sugar
1 bay leaf
½ teaspoon black peppercorns
1 teaspoon coarse salt
2 teaspoons fennel seeds
1 tablespoon coriander seeds
1 teaspoon mustard seeds
¼ teaspoon red pepper flakes
2 strips lemon zest

1] If the mushrooms are small, keep them whole. Cut larger ones in halves or quarters and reserve.

2] Combine all the ingredients except the mushrooms in a medium saucepan with 2 cups water. Bring to a boil, reduce to a simmer, and cook, covered, 10 minutes.

3] Add the mushrooms, pressing down with a spoon so they are all covered by liquid. Cook over medium heat 10 minutes, uncovered. With a slotted spoon, transfer the mushrooms along with any seasonings that are clinging to them, to a plastic container.

4] Turn the heat up to high and reduce the liquid by rapidly boiling for 10 minutes. Strain over the mushrooms in the container and let sit till cool, about 2 hours. Cover and chill at least 8 hours before serving.

EGG AND CHEESE DISHES

EGGS ARE TAKEN SERIOUSLY IN FRANCE, WHERE THEY ARE NOT EATEN SO MUCH AS A BREAKFAST FOOD BUT INCORPORATED INTO LUNCH AND DINNER MENUS IN THE FORM OF OMELETTES, SOUFFLÉS, QUICHES, AND SUCH CLASSIC APPETIZERS AS SOFTLY SCRAMBLED EGGS TOPPED WITH CAVIAR. AS FOR THE SINCERITY BROUGHT TO COOKING THIS HUMBLE INGREDIENT PROPERLY, WHOLE TREATISES HAVE BEEN WRITTEN ON THE PREPARATION AND ENJOYMENT OF A PERFECT OMELETTE.

ASPARAGUS QUICHE

Granted, quiche sounds old, overexposed, and just too eggy, but I am hard pressed to come up with anything better for weekend brunch. It can be made ahead, served from a buffet at room temperature, and simplified even more by substituting a prepared pie shell. Asparagus and eggs make an especially nice combination. ✻ *Serves 6 to 8*

1 recipe Pâte Brisée (page 107)
1½ teaspoons salt
1 pound asparagus, washed, ends trimmed, and cut on the diagonal into ½-inch lengths
1 tablespoon unsalted butter

1 medium onion, peeled and diced
3 jumbo eggs
½ cup heavy cream
¾ cup grated Gruyère or Swiss cheese
Freshly ground black pepper

1] Preheat oven to 375 F. Line a 10-inch tart pan with pâte brisée and place in the refrigerator for 30 minutes. Prick the bottom with the tines of a fork, cover with a sheet of aluminum foil or parchment paper, and fill with rice, dried beans, or pie weights. Bake 10 minutes, remove the lining and weights, and set aside.

2] Bring a medium saucepan of water to a boil. Add ½ teaspoon of the salt and the asparagus and cook 2 minutes once the water returns to a boil. Strain, transfer to a bowl of cold water to stop the cooking, and strain again. Pat dry with paper towels.

3] In a medium skillet, melt the butter over medium heat. Cook the onion for 5 minutes to soften. Then add the asparagus and ½ teaspoon more of the salt and continue cooking, stirring occasionally, 10 minutes longer. Remove from the heat.

4] In a large mixing bowl, whisk together the eggs, cream, and ½ cup of the cheese. Add the asparagus mixture and stir well to combine. Mix in the remaining ½ teaspoon of salt and season with black pepper to taste.

5] Pour the mixture into the prebaked tart shell and sprinkle the remaining cheese over the top. Place on a baking sheet or cookie tray and bake until golden brown and puffy, about 40 minutes. Set aside to cool 10 minutes, transfer to a serving platter, and serve warm or at room temperature.

SAVORY LEEK TART

This northern version of quiche, called a flamiche, adapted from a recipe in Patricia Wells's book *Bistro Cooking*, is a favorite for casual suppers and brunches. I like to serve it accompanied with bitter greens, good black olives, and sliced tomatoes. ✘ *Serves 6 to 8*

1 recipe Pâte Brisée (page 107)
3 pounds leeks
4 tablespoons (½ stick) unsalted
   butter
Salt
Black pepper

3 large eggs
½ cup heavy cream
¾ cup grated Parmesan cheese
3 or 4 small marinated sun-dried
   tomatoes, cut into thin strips

1] Line a 10-inch tart shell with pâte brisée and chill while preparing the filling.

2] Trim off the root ends and green stalks of the leeks and cut the white sections in half lengthwise. Under cold running water rinse out the sand between the layers. Then cut each half into long strips and cut across the strips to chop roughly.

3] Melt the butter over medium-low heat in your largest skillet, preferably 14 inches in diameter. Add the leeks, salt, and pepper and cook, covered, stirring occasionally, until soft, about 30 minutes.

4] Preheat the oven to 425 F.

5] In a mixing bowl, whisk together the eggs, cream, and ½ cup of the Parmesan cheese. Add the leeks and mix well to combine. Pour into the unbaked tart shell. Sprinkle the top with the remaining ¼ cup cheese and ground pepper and arrange the strips of sun-dried tomatoes in a spoke pattern.

6] Bake until well-browned, 30 to 40 minutes. Set aside to cool 10 minutes before serving.

Omelette with Wild Mushrooms and Scallions

Omelette-making does require some practice, so if your eggs look as if they are not about to cooperate, just scramble them and try again another time. The flavor will still be delicious. ✖ *Serves 1*

2 eggs
½ teaspoon sesame oil
Salt
White pepper
2 large fresh shiitake mushrooms, caps only, wiped clean

3 scallions including 1 inch of the green
1½ tablespoons unsalted butter
¼ teaspoon sliced fresh chives

1] In a small bowl, beat the eggs, sesame oil, salt, and pepper together with a fork just until blended.

2] Cut the mushroom caps into large chunks, and finely chop the scallions.

3] Melt 1 tablespoon of the butter in an 8-inch skillet (preferably a well-seasoned cast-iron one) over high heat. Sauté the mushrooms and scallions just until their aromas are released and the butter absorbed, about 1½ minutes. Tip the vegetables out into a bowl.

4] Return the pan to high heat and melt the remaining ½ tablespoon of butter. Pour in the beaten eggs, quickly swirling the pan to coat it evenly. As soon as the bottom is set, reduce the heat to medium-high and start shaking the pan back and forth to prevent sticking. Sprinkle the sautéed mushrooms and scallions over the center and with a fork or spoon lift an edge and fold over to partially enclose the filling. Continue cooking, shaking the pan frequently, about a minute, and then tilt out onto a plate. Sprinkle chives over the top and serve.

EGGS EN COCOTTE

What could be simpler or better than eggs baked with a dollop of cream? They are a natural for serving breakfast to a group since they all come out of the oven together. ✗ *Serves 4*

2 teaspoons butter
16 teaspoons heavy cream
Salt and pepper

8 cold eggs
8 Italian parsley leaves
8 slices toasted bread

1] Preheat the oven to 400 F.

2] Lightly butter the bottom and sides of eight ½-cup ovenproof ramekins or custard cups. Swirl 1 teaspoon of cream in the bottom of each and sprinkle with salt and pepper. One at a time, break the eggs into a cup and slide them into the ramekins, being careful not to disturb the yolks. Top each with another teaspoon of cream. Transfer ramekins to a roasting pan.

3] Bring a kettle of water nearly to a boil and then carefully pour hot water into the roasting pan so it comes halfway up the sides of the ramekins. Transfer pan to the oven and bake until the whites are opaque and the yolks just set, 8 to 10 minutes.

4] Spread a kitchen towel on the counter and, using pot holders or a towel, remove the ramekins and place on the towel to dry the bottoms. Garnish each with a parsley leaf. Place the ramekins on larger plates and serve with toast.

POULTRY, MEAT, AND FISH

In attempting to streamline and modernize many of the favorites of the French country kitchen, one ingredient that could not be eliminated was time— especially that required for cooking the meats. Getting the best from inexpensive cuts like lamb shank or shoulder, or melding the flavors for a decent cassoulet or boeuf bourguignon, does take a few hours. They repay you, however, with wonderfully dense flavors and terrific leftovers. When you need to get out of the kitchen fast, with something great to show for it, try Peppered Swordfish with Olives and Lemon (page 74), Inauthentic Bouillabaise (page 69), or Veal Chops with Apples and Thyme (page 54). All can be on the table in less than 30 minutes.

CHICKEN WITH 40 CLOVES OF GARLIC AND FRESH HERBS

In this classic chicken dish from Provence, the entire bird is subtly suffused with the fragrance of garlic, herbs, and olive oil. Whatever you do, do not skip the toasted bread. It is a must for savoring every last bit of sweet roasted garlic. Lovers of crisp skin be warned—this skin remains soft since the bird is braised. *Serves 4*

One 3½- to 4-pound chicken
Salt
Freshly ground black pepper
1 cup olive oil
5 heads garlic, cloves separated and peeled

4 bunches (about 4 cups) mixed fresh herbs, such as basil, parsley, rosemary, thyme, tarragon, and marjoram
1 loaf French or Italian bread, cut in ½-inch slices

1] Preheat the oven to 400 F. Wash the chicken and pat dry. Sprinkle inside and out with salt and pepper.

2] Pour ½ cup of the olive oil into a large roasting pan. In a single layer in the center of the pan, arrange ¾ of the garlic cloves. Stuff the remaining garlic cloves and half of the fresh herbs, stems and all, in the chicken's cavity. Place the chicken, breast side up, over the bed of garlic.

3] Place the remaining herbs on top of the chicken and pour the remaining olive oil over all. Cover (improvise with aluminum foil if you do not have a lid) and bake 1 hour. Remove from oven and let sit, with the cover on, ½ hour before serving. Do not turn the oven off.

4] Place the bread slices on a baking tray and toast in the hot oven about 6 minutes per side.

5] To serve, remove the herbs and garlic from the chicken's cavity, cut the bird into serving pieces, and transfer to a platter. Brush the slices of toasted bread with the garlic-infused oil from the pan and scatter around the edges of the platter. Transfer the garlic cloves to a serving bowl—they are delicious either spread on the toast, eaten with the chicken, or combined with mashed potatoes as in the recipe on page 77.

CHICKEN IN THE POT WITH WINTER VEGETABLES

══════ ■ ══════

The true poule au pot, from southwestern France, is a much more elaborate dish calling for meat stuffing and hard-boiled egg sauce. This quicker version, however, has its virtues: It is a low-fat, one-dish meal that provides double density chicken stock for the rest of the week. It is worth beginning with homemade chicken stock for such a clean, pure dish. ✗ *Serves 6*

3 turnips, trimmed and peeled
4 carrots, trimmed and peeled
3 celery ribs, trimmed
3 leeks, trimmed, white part only halved lengthwise and cleaned
4 pounds chicken breast halves and thighs, with bone and skin
3 bay leaves

¼ cup fresh chopped tarragon, or 1 tablespoon dried
3 whole cloves
¼ teaspoon fennel seeds
1 teaspoon salt
½ teaspoon white pepper
6 cups homemade chicken stock
2 cups dry white wine

1] Wash all the vegetables and cut into 2- by ¼-inch matchsticks or julienne. Mix together in a large bowl. Wash the chicken pieces and pat them dry.

2] Divide the vegetable mixture in half and place half in the bottom of your largest stockpot. Top with 2 bay leaves and then the chicken pieces. Scatter the remaining vegetables over the chicken. Sprinkle on the tarragon, cloves, fennel seed, salt, and pepper. Pour in the chicken stock and wine.

3] Bring to a boil, reduce to a simmer, and skim the foam that rises to the top. Cover and cook 45 minutes. Using tongs or slotted spoons, transfer the chicken to a platter. Strain the broth into a large bowl. Discard the bay leaves and place the warm vegetables either in the bottom of a soup tureen or in 6 pasta plates or deep soup bowls. Keep warm in a 200 F oven.

4] Pour the strained broth back into the stockpot. Cook at a lively boil, uncovered 20 minutes longer to reduce the liquid and concentrate the flavors. Check the pot occasionally and, with a ladle, skim off and discard the fat that gathers at the edges of the pot. Taste and adjust seasonings with salt and pepper—a densely flavored, golden broth should result.

5] You may want to remove the chicken skin before serving. Place chicken pieces over the vegetables in the tureen or serving bowls and return to the oven for 5 minutes. Ladle on the broth and serve hot with crusty French bread.

COQ AU VIN

Coq au vin, or chicken stewed in red wine with mushrooms and pearl onions, is surely one of the world's best known chicken dishes. The original recipe, dating back to the Romans, called for a year-old rooster, with its liver, heart, and blood used to enrich the sauce. These days you can substitute a beurre manié—a paste made of butter and flour—for thickening. ✖ *Serves 6 to 8*

5 ounces or 1 cup white pearl
  onions, roots trimmed
6 pounds chicken breasts and
  thighs, with skin and bone
Salt
Freshly ground black pepper
6 tablespoons all-purpose flour
4 tablespoons (½ stick) unsalted
  butter
4 ounces salt pork or slab bacon,
  trimmed and cut into ½- by
  ½- by ¼-inch pieces
8 ounces whole white mushrooms,
  wiped clean with a damp paper
  towel

1 large carrot, peeled, trimmed,
  and sliced
2 garlic cloves, peeled and crushed
1 tablespoon tomato paste
¼ cup Cognac
1 bottle red wine
2 tablespoons chopped fresh thyme
3 bay leaves
2 tablespoons unsalted butter,
  softened
2 tablespoons flour

1] Bring a small saucepan of water to a boil and add the onions. Cook for 3 minutes and then rinse with cold water to stop the cooking; this removes the onion's harshness and makes peeling easier. Squeeze the onions to remove the skins and set aside.

2] Wash the chicken parts and pat dry. Chop each breast half in half again. Sprinkle all over with salt and pepper. Spread 6 tablespoons flour on a platter and dredge each piece of chicken to coat thoroughly. Pat off excess flour.

3] In a large heavy pot or dutch oven over moderate heat, cook 4 tablespoons butter with the salt pork or bacon until brown, about 7 minutes. Add the chicken and brown in batches, about 3 minutes per side. Transfer the chicken and bacon to a platter near the stove.

4] Add the blanched, peeled onions, mushrooms, carrots, garlic, and tomato paste to the pot. Sauté, stirring frequently, until the mushrooms brown, about 5 minutes. Pour in the Cognac and continue cooking at high heat, scraping and stirring up the browned bits from the bottom of the pan, until the bottom is nearly dry.

5] Put the chicken and bacon back in the pot. Pour in the wine, thyme, and bay leaves and stir well to distribute the flavors. (Do not season with salt and pepper now because the sauce will later be reduced to concentrate its flavors.) Bring to a boil, reduce to a simmer and cook, covered, 1 hour.

6] Using slotted spoons, transfer the chicken, mushrooms, onions, and carrots to a large platter or roasting pan. Bring the liquids in the pot to a boil over high heat and continue cooking, uncovered, about 5 minutes to reduce and concentrate the flavors. With a ladle, remove and discard the fat that rises to the top. Remove and discard the bay leaves.

7] Reduce the heat to low. Mix the softened butter and flour together to make a paste, called a beurre manié. Press it onto the ends of a whisk and slowly whisk into the sauce until smooth. Season to taste with salt and pepper. Return the chicken and vegetables to the pot and continue cooking another few minutes just to heat through. Serve hot with plenty of crusty bread, plain rice, or noodles for the sauce.

CHICKEN LEGS WITH VINEGAR AND TARRAGON

The French have a hundred variations on sautéed chicken. This is one of my favorites—chicken simmered in a pungent sauce of vinegar, shallots, and tarragon. It is an easy one-skillet supper that asks for nothing more than a fresh baguette to soak up the juices. ✄ *Serves 4 to 6*

6 chicken legs with thighs
Salt
Freshly ground black pepper
4 tablespoons (½ stick) unsalted
   butter
1 tablespoon olive oil
1 cup white wine vinegar

½ cup chopped shallots (about 3
   large shallots)
¾ cup chicken stock
2 tomatoes, peeled, seeded, and
   diced (see page 27)
2 tablespoons chopped fresh
   tarragon

1] Wash the chicken pieces, pat dry, and generously season with salt and pepper.

2] Melt 2 tablespoons of the butter with the olive oil in a large skillet over medium-high heat. Sauté the chicken until brown on both sides, about 7 minutes per side. Transfer to a platter and carefully pour off the fat in the pan. (Do not wipe clean. The browned bits on the bottom will add flavor to the sauce.)

3] Reduce the heat to low and slowly pour in the vinegar, standing back to avoid the fumes. Add the shallots, turn the heat to medium, and stir and scrape the bottom of the pan to loosen the bits. Continue boiling to reduce the vinegar by half, about 7 minutes. (The shallots should be well coated and a medium pool of vinegar should remain in the pan.)

4] Pour in the chicken stock and tomatoes and return the chicken to the pan, skin side down. Reduce the heat to medium-low, cover, and cook 10 minutes per side. Then transfer the cooked chicken to a platter.

5] Reduce the heat to low. Cut the remaining 2 tablespoons of butter into 4 pieces. Finish the sauce by stirring in the tarragon and butter with a wooden spoon until the butter is just melted. Taste for salt and pepper (salt will offset vinegar's acidity), spoon the sauce over the chicken, and serve hot.

CRISP
ROASTED CHICKEN

Every home cook needs one absolutely foolproof roast chicken recipe for those times when takeout chicken is just not good enough. I learned this technique—stuffing the chicken under the skin with butter, garlic, and herbs and roasting at high heat—from cooking teacher Renée Carisio, who learned it from Jacques Pépin. It produces a perfectly moist chicken covered with crackling brown skin, my family's favorite Sunday night supper. ✕ *Serves 4*

One 4-pound chicken
3 tablespoons unsalted butter, softened
1 garlic clove, peeled and minced
3 tablespoons finely chopped fresh herbs such as sage, parsley, rosemary, thyme, tarragon, and basil

Salt
Freshly ground black pepper

1] Preheat the oven to 425 F.

2] Remove and discard everything in the bird's cavity and rinse with cold water inside and out. Pat dry and sprinkle the inside with salt and pepper. Trim and discard any excess fat and skin from the tail and neck area. Place breast up on a counter.

3] In a small bowl, use a fork to mash the butter with the garlic and herbs to form a paste.

4] Loosen the skin by carefully lifting the area around the neck and gently running your index finger between the skin and meat along the breasts and legs. Divide the butter and herb paste into 4 parts. Stuff one portion into each breast and leg and spread it by pressing the skin to flatten the paste. Sprinkle the outside generously with salt and pepper.

5] Place the bird on its side in a roasting pan and roast 20 minutes; turn bird to other side and roast 20 minutes more. Then roast 20 minutes breast side up. (Be sure to use pot holders, tongs, or a large slotted spoon to turn the bird; the fat in the pan is very hot. Use a brush or spoon to baste after each turning.) Transfer to a cutting board and let cool 15 minutes before carving and serving.

VEAL BLANQUETTE

Blanquette de veau is a simple stew of veal in its own cooking juices thickened with egg yolks and cream and finished with a dash of lemon juice. It is excellent on a bed of rice or noodles with a green salad on the side. ✗ *Serves 4*

2 pounds veal for stewing, from the rump or breast
2 large carrots, peeled and cut in 2-inch lengths
4 whole cloves
1 large onion, peeled
1 large celery rib, washed and cut in half
4 thyme sprigs
1 bay leaf
1 large rosemary sprig

4 parsley sprigs
½ teaspoon black peppercorns
1 teaspoon salt
3 egg yolks
¼ cup heavy cream
2 tablespoons unsalted butter
2 tablespoons all-purpose flour
2 tablespoons lemon juice
2 tablespoons chopped fresh Italian parsley
1 tablespoon drained capers

1] Wash the meat, trim into 1-inch cubes, and place in the bottom of a large dutch oven or heavy saucepan along with the carrots. Press the cloves into the onion and add to the pot.

2] Make a bouquet garni: In the hollow of half a celery stalk, place the thyme and bay leaf. Fold the rosemary and parsley sprigs in half to fit and add to the thyme and bay leaf. Cover with the other celery half and then tie with kitchen string (dental floss is a good substitute) to enclose the herbs. Set in the pot with the meat.

3] Pour in just enough cold water to cover, about 3½ cups, add the peppercorns and salt, and bring almost to a boil. Skim and discard the foam that rises to the top. Cover and cook at the lowest possible simmer for 1 hour. Turn off the heat and let the meat cool in the pot, with the cover on, for ½ hour.

4] Using a slotted spoon, transfer the meat and carrots to a bowl. Strain the broth into another bowl, removing and discarding the bouquet garni.

5] Whisk together the egg yolks and cream in a small bowl and have that and the remaining ingredients ready near the stove.

6] To make the sauce, melt the butter over medium-low heat in a medium saucepan. Add the flour and continue cooking over low heat, stirring constantly with a wooden spoon, until the mixture turns thick and smooth and loses the taste of flour, about 2 minutes. Gradually pour in the reserved veal broth, whisking continuously over low heat to eliminate lumps. Turn the heat up to high and boil for 5 minutes to thicken the sauce. Skim and discard any foam or grease that rises to the top.

7] Turn off the heat and slowly whisk 1 cup of hot broth into the reserved egg yolk mixture. Slowly pour the egg mixture back into the broth and cook over low heat, whisking constantly. Whisk in the lemon juice, parsley, and capers and taste for salt and pepper. Return the meat and carrots to the pot and cook for another minute over low heat to avoid curdling, just to heat through. Serve hot.

VEAL CHOPS WITH
APPLES AND THYME

∎

Veal with apples and cream is a typical dish of Normandy, the northern home of the best butter, cream, and apple brandy. This elegant dish is deceptively quick. ✖ *Serves 4*

4 tablespoons (½ stick) unsalted
    butter
4 small Golden Delicious apples,
    cored, peeled, and cut into
    8 wedges each
1 teaspoon fresh chopped thyme
Juice of 1 lemon

Salt
Freshly ground black pepper
Four 6-ounce veal loin chops
2 tablespoons Calvados, applejack,
    or pear brandy
¼ cup heavy cream

1] Melt 2 tablespoons butter in a medium skillet over medium-high heat. Sauté the apples with thyme until golden brown, about 8 minutes. Stir in the lemon juice and transfer mixture to 4 serving plates.

2] While the apples are cooking, salt and pepper the veal chops. Melt the remaining butter in a large skillet over medium-high heat. Cook the veal chops about 4 minutes per side. Remove from heat and transfer the chops to the serving plates, over the apples.

3] Pour the brandy into the skillet used for cooking the veal and return to moderate heat. Scrape the bottom of the pan with a wooden spoon to loosen the browned bits, and then swirl in the cream. Reduce over high heat, stirring and scraping, until the sauce is brown and thick, a minute or two. Spoon over the meat and serve hot.

ROAST PORK WITH SHALLOTS AND HONEY

Savory mustard and sweet honey bring out the best in this simply roasted meat. In the summertime I like to serve an easy dish like this at room temperature. ✕ *Serves 4*

2 pounds boneless pork loin roast
Salt
Freshly ground black pepper
2 tablespoons olive oil
⅓ cup Dijon mustard
14 shallots, peeled

6 sage leaves, or 6 sprigs fresh
  thyme
About 1 cup white wine
½ cup chicken stock or pan juices
2 tablespoons honey
2 teaspoons fresh lemon juice

1] Preheat the oven to 425 F.

2] Wash and pat dry the meat and generously sprinkle with salt and pepper.

3] Combine the olive oil and mustard in a small bowl to make a paste and rub all over the roast. Place roast in the center of a small roasting pan. Scatter the shallots and sage leaves over the meat and in the bottom of the pan.

4] Pour in the wine to a depth of about ½ inch and roast, uncovered, 1 hour and 15 minutes. Check every half hour or so, adding a half cup of wine if the pan is dry and basting the meat with a spoon or brush. Transfer the finished roast to a cutting board and let rest 10 minutes before slicing. Reserve the roasted shallots.

5] Make a sauce by combining chicken stock or pan juices and honey in a small saucepan. Bring to a boil and cook over high heat, stirring occasionally, about 4 minutes. Skim and discard any foam that rises to the top. Reduce the heat to low, stir in lemon juice, and remove from heat.

6] Carve the pork roast into ¼-inch slices across the width and fan on a platter. Garnish with roasted shallots. Pour the sauce over all and serve.

LAMB BROCHETTES PROVENÇAL

Fresh rosemary sprigs tossed on the coals right before grilling will give a boost to these sprightly lamb brochettes from Provence. ✕ *Serves 4*

¼ cup chopped fresh rosemary
2 garlic cloves, peeled and crushed
½ cup olive oil
½ cup lemon juice
½ teaspoon cracked black pepper
1 teaspoon salt
8 rib lamb chops, trimmed off the
   bone and cut into chunks
   (reserve bones for stock and
   soup-making)

1 lemon, washed and cut into
   8 small wedges
1 onion, peeled and cut into
   8 small wedges
4 ripe plum tomatoes

1] Whisk together the rosemary, garlic, olive oil, lemon juice, pepper, and salt in a shallow noncorrosive pan. Add the chunks of meat, toss with the marinade, and cover. Marinate in the refrigerator for 8 hours.

2] Preheat the grill or broiler.

3] Make 8 small skewers, alternating the lemon wedges, onion wedges, and meat, with a plum tomato in the center of each. (If you are using bamboo skewers, be sure to soak them first for 30 minutes to avoid having them splinter on the grill.)

4] Grill, covered, over medium heat, or 4 inches from the heat in the broiler, for 13 minutes total. Use tongs to turn the skewers every few minutes for even cooking. Serve hot.

ROAST LEG OF LAMB WITH HERBS, OLIVES, AND GARLIC

L amb's gaminess is balanced by lots of garlic and fresh herbs in this easy stuffing for butterflied leg of lamb. The French prefer to eat lamb very rare, or *saignant.* Just increase the cooking time accordingly if you prefer it better done. ✗ *Serves 6 to 8*

½ cup mixed chopped fresh herbs such as basil, mint, rosemary, chives, parsley, thyme, and oregano

2 tablespoons finely minced garlic

2 tablespoons olive oil

⅓ cup Kalamata olives, sliced off pits and chopped

One 5-pound leg of lamb (ask the butcher to remove bones, excess sinew, and fat, and butterfly for stuffing)

Salt

Freshly ground black pepper

Olive oil

1] Preheat the oven to 450 F.

2] Make a paste by combing the herbs, garlic, olive oil, and olives in a small bowl and mixing with a spoon.

3] Lay the lamb on the counter, interior facing up, and score the meat several times with a sharp blade so the flavoring will penetrate. Generously sprinkle with salt and pepper. Spread the garlic herb paste over the meat with your fingers and then roll to enclose the stuffing. Tie with string in about 3 places across the roll and skewer, if necessary, to seal. Sprinkle the outside with salt and pepper and drizzle with olive oil.

4] Place on a rack in a roasting pan and roast for 15 minutes. Then reduce the temperature to 350 F and continue roasting 50 minutes longer for medium-rare. Let rest at room temperature 10 minutes before carving. Remove the strings and slice thinly across the width. Serve warm.

BRAISED LAMB SHANKS

There is something about having a couple of shank bones on the kitchen counter, as opposed to boneless chicken breasts, that puts you directly in touch with the elements. Now you are really cooking! What a great winter dish to serve over a bed of warm couscous or orzo, along with a good bottle of red wine. ✗ *Serves 4*

4 lamb shanks
Salt
Freshly ground black pepper
1 cup all-purpose flour
2 tablespoons vegetable oil
2 tablespoons unsalted butter
1 large onion, peeled and chopped
2 celery ribs, chopped
1 large carrot, peeled and chopped

3 garlic cloves, peeled and crushed
1 cup dry white wine
1 quart beef or chicken stock
¼ cup chopped fresh oregano, or
   1 tablespoon dried
¼ teaspoon cayenne
¼ teaspoon ground cumin
Grated zest of 1 orange

1] Preheat the oven to 350 F.

2] Sprinkle the lamb shanks all over with salt and pepper. Place the flour in a bowl. Dip each shank to coat with flour and pat off excess.

3] Heat the oil and the butter in a large skillet over high heat. Brown the shanks on all sides and then transfer to a large roasting pan, where they should fit comfortably.

4] Reduce the heat in the skillet to medium and add the onion, celery, carrot, and garlic. Sauté, stirring frequently, until the vegetables begin to color, about 8 minutes. Then pour in the wine. Turn the heat up to high and cook until only a small pool of wine remains in the pan. Add the stock, oregano, cayenne, cumin, and ½ teaspoon salt and bring to a boil. Pour over the shanks in the pan. (Add water, if necessary, to barely cover.) Cover and bake 2½ hours, or until the meat easily falls off the bone. Skim and discard any fat that has risen to the top, sprinkle in the orange zest, and serve the shanks hot in their cooking juices.

STEAK AU POIVRE

Steak in peppercorn crust accompanied by a mound of french-fried potatoes is a standard of brasseries and bistros all over France. The steak is an easy dish to prepare at home for you and your favorite carnivore.

Serves 2

Two 10-ounce rib eye, sirloin, or spencer steaks
Salt
4 teaspoons cracked black peppercorns
1 teaspoon vegetable oil
2 tablespoons plus 1 teaspoon unsalted butter
2 tablespoons Cognac or brandy
½ cup beef stock

1] Sprinkle the steaks all over with salt. Spread 1 teaspoon of peppercorns over each side of each steak and press with your fingertips to make the peppercorns stick. Let sit 20 minutes for the flavor to penetrate.

2] Heat the oil with 1 teaspoon of the butter in a large skillet over high heat. When the butter melts, add the steaks and cook over high heat, 4 minutes per side for rare, 6 minutes each side for medium rare. Transfer the steaks to serving plates.

3] Off the heat, pour the Cognac or brandy into the pan, and then return to high heat. (The heat in the pan will cause the alcohol to evaporate almost immediately.) Pour in the beef stock and cook at a rapid boil about 4 minutes. Remove from heat and add the 2 tablespoons butter a small piece at a time, constantly stirring with a wooden spoon. Pour over the meat and serve.

Boeuf Bourguignon

From Burgundy, the region known for its great home cooking, its beef, and its wine, comes this classic beef stewed in red wine. The trick to keeping the meat juicy and tender is to start with large enough chunks of a fatty cut like chuck or rump and not to rush the cooking. Serve with a plain accompaniment like boiled potatoes, rice, or noodles. *Serves 4*

12 pearl or small white boiling onions
2 tablespoons vegetable oil
4 tablespoons (1/2 stick) unsalted butter
1/4 pound salt pork or thickly sliced bacon, cut in 1/4-inch strips
3 garlic cloves, peeled and minced
2 1/2 pounds chuck, rump, or sirloin tip roast
Salt
Freshly ground black pepper
8 small carrots, trimmed, peeled, and cut in half lengthwise and then across the width
Bouquet garni of 6 sprigs each parsley and thyme and 2 bay leaves
1 tablespoon all-purpose flour
2 teaspoons tomato paste
2 cups red wine
1/2 pound small white mushrooms, stems trimmed and wiped clean (optional)
Juice of 1/2 lemon

1] Bring a small saucepan of water to a boil. Trim the root ends of the onions and blanch in the boiling water for 3 minutes. Rinse with cold water and then squeeze to remove the skins.

2] Cut the beef into generous 2- by 3-inch chunks, following the natural separations. Pat thoroughly dry with paper towels. Sprinkle all over with salt and pepper.

3] Heat the oil and 2 tablespoons butter in a large dutch oven or heavy pot over medium heat. Cook the onions, salt pork or bacon, and garlic, stirring frequently, until the pork begins to brown, about 5 minutes.

4] Turn the heat up to high and cook the meat in batches until well browned on all sides. Return all the meat to the pan.

5] Preheat the oven to 300 F.

6] Add the carrots and bouquet garni. Reduce the heat to low, cover, and cook 15 minutes. Check the pot and stir once or twice to avoid sticking. With a slotted spoon or tongs, transfer the meat, pork or bacon, and bouquet garni to a platter near the stove.

7] Gradually sprinkle the flour into the pan, stirring constantly. When the flour disappears and the sauce is smooth, stir in the tomato paste. Slowly add the wine, stirring constantly, and raise the heat to high. Bring nearly to a boil. Return the beef, pork, and bouquet garni to the pot. Cover and bake in the oven for 3 hours.

8] If using the mushrooms, melt the remaining 2 tablespoons butter in a medium skillet over high heat. Sauté the whole mushrooms until they being to brown and the butter is absorbed, 4 minutes. Sprinkle with lemon juice. Stir into the finished stew. Remove the bouquet garni and serve.

POT AU FEU

Pot au feu, the famous French boiled beef dinner, is meditative weekend cooking at its best. Though there is nothing difficult about it, it demands several hours of intermittent attention and tender loving care. It then rewards you with mountains of homely boiled beef, glazed winter vegetables, and bowlfuls of restorative beef broth. Over the years a repertoire of recipes have developed for reenergizing the leftovers, although I find sandwiches with rye bread, mustard, and horseradish just fine. ✖ *Serves 6 to 8*

4 to 5 pounds beef, such as chuck, brisket, or short ribs
1½ pounds beef bones (optional)
1 onion, peeled
2 cloves
1 carrot, peeled and cut into 2-inch lengths
2 celery ribs, trimmed and cut into 2-inch lengths
2 bay leaves
12 parsley sprigs
12 thyme sprigs
½ teaspoon black peppercorns

1 teaspoon salt
6 white boiling potatoes, peeled and reserved in a bowl of cold water
6 large carrots, peeled, trimmed and cut into 4-inch lengths
6 leeks, white part only, trimmed, halved lengthwise, and thoroughly washed
Salt
Freshly ground black pepper
Mustard, horseradish, and pickles or cornichons

1] Place the beef and bones in a large stockpot. Pierce the onion with the cloves and add to the pot along with the sliced carrot, celery, and bay leaves. Tie the herb sprigs together with string for easy removal and place them and the peppercorns in the pot. Add enough cold water to cover and bring just barely to a boil, over medium heat. Reduce the heat to low. (You don't want the water to really boil because that would toughen the meat's fibers. Very slow cooking results in tenderer meat.) Cook, uncovered, 3½ hours, or until the meat feels soft when pierced with a fork. Occasionally skim and discard the foam and scum that rises to the top.

2] Transfer the finished meat to a platter or deep bowl and cover with foil. Keep warm in a 200 F oven. Using your finest strainer, or a strainer lined with cheesecloth, strain the stock, discarding the solids. If you have the time, refrigerate the stock about 2 hours so the fat rises to the top; otherwise just ladle off the fat as best you can. (This is a good time to take a natural break in the recipe, if you are cooking in advance. Just refrigerate the meat and stock separately and reheat the meat along with 1 cup of stock in a 325 F oven before serving.)

3] Bring a large saucepan of water to a boil. Add salt and the potatoes and cook at a moderate boil 10 minutes. Add the carrots and leeks and cook another 10 minutes. Transfer the vegetables to a large skillet along with ¾ cup of the reserved beef broth. Cook at a low boil until the liquid has evaporated.

4] Meanwhile pour the remaining stock into a saucepan. Bring to a boil and cook about 10 minutes to reduce. Add salt and pepper to taste.

5] To serve, thinly slice the brisket or chuck across the grain, or slice the short ribs off the bone. Arrange on a deep platter along with the vegetables. Moisten with a few ladlefuls of stock and bring to the table, along with a bowl of the remaining stock, mustards, horseradish, pickles, coarse salt, and a pepper mill for adding at the table.

FAUX CASSOULET

This abbreviated version of the classic meat and bean casserole from Languedoc eliminates such hard-to-find or high-fat ingredients as duck confit, goose fat, and pork rind in favor of supermarket ingredients like chicken thighs and sausage. This is a wonderful slow dish to cook on a winter weekend and serve throughout the week. ✖ *Serves 6*

1 pound dry white beans, such as
    Great Northern or cannellini
Sprig of rosemary
2 tablespoons vegetable oil
4 spicy pork sausages, such as
    Italian, Cajun, or Polish
    kielbasa, cut in 2-inch lengths
2 pounds chicken thighs, with skin
    and bone
1 pound boneless lamb shoulder
    meat, cut in 1½-inch chunks

Salt
Freshly ground black pepper
2 medium onions, peeled and
    diced
10 small garlic cloves, peeled and
    crushed
3 cups chicken stock, reserved bean
    liquid, or a combination
Juice of ½ lemon
1½ cups dry bread crumbs

1] Place the beans in a colander and rinse with cold water. Transfer them to a large heavy saucepan, cover generously with water, add the rosemary sprig, and bring to a boil. Reduce to a simmer and cook, covered, until the beans are soft, about 2 hours. Strain and reserve the beans and liquid.

2] Heat the vegetable oil in a large skillet over medium-high heat. Cook the sausage until lightly browned, about 6 minutes, and transfer to a platter. Carefully pour off all but about 3 tablespoons of fat from the pan. Salt and pepper the chicken and lamb pieces. Brown them in batches in the same skillet and transfer to the platter. In the same skillet, sauté the onions and garlic over medium heat until soft, about 10 minutes. Stir and scrape the browned bits from the bottom of the pan to loosen.

3] Preheat the oven to 325 F.

4] In a large casserole or roasting pan, spread half of the beans. Layer the various meats snugly over the beans and top with the onion garlic mixture. Cover with the remaining beans and pour in the chicken stock or bean broth.

5] Transfer to the oven and bake, covered, 2 hours. Remove from oven and turn the heat up to 350 F. (Check the liquid in the pan. It should be moist but not swimming in liquid. If necessary, use a small ladle to spoon off excess liquid.) Drizzle the casserole with lemon juice. Sprinkle with a thick even layer of bread crumbs and return to the oven to bake, uncovered, until browned, 1 hour. Serve hot.

HACHIS PARMENTIER

This standard French homemaker's dish resembles a meat pie with a bottom and top crust of mashed potatoes. It makes a lovely casual supper with a green salad, a loaf of bread, and some red wine. Be sure to break into the crisp top crust at the table—the steam is heavenly. Hachis can be made in advance and reheated. ✖ *Serves 4*

2 pounds baking potatoes, washed
6 tablespoons (³/₄ stick) unsalted butter
2 tablespoons vegetable oil
4 garlic cloves, peeled and minced
1 medium onion, peeled and diced
1½ pounds chopped sirloin

2½ teaspoons salt
Freshly ground black pepper
1 cup low-fat milk
¼ cup chopped fresh parsley
3 tablespoons grated Parmesan or Gruyère cheese

1] Coat a 9-inch Pyrex pie plate with a teaspoon of butter.

2] Fill a large saucepan with cold water. Peel the potatoes, cut into large chunks, and place in the pot of water. Bring to a boil and cook over high heat, uncovered, until soft, about 20 minutes.

3] Meanwhile heat the oil and 1 tablespoon of the butter in a large skillet over moderate heat. Sauté the garlic and onion until soft, about 7 minutes. Then add the meat, 1½ teaspoons of the salt, and ground pepper to taste. Turn the heat up to high, and cook another 10 minutes, frequently turning and break up with a spoon to brown the meat evenly.

4] Heat the milk and 4 tablespoons of the butter in a small saucepan over moderate heat. Do not bring to a boil.

5] Preheat the oven to 350 F.

6] When the potatoes are soft, drain them, leaving the potatoes in the pan. Mash with a potato masher, fork, or ricer and place over low heat. Slowly pour in the hot milk and butter mixture, mixing and mashing until well combined. Mix in 1 teaspoon of salt and a generous quantity of black pepper.

7] Spread half of the mashed potatoes on the bottom of the coated pie plate. (A spatula with a butter knife does the job well.) Using a slotted spoon to drain the meat, spread it over the potatoes and then sprinkle with the parsley. Top with the remaining potatoes, sprinkle with grated cheese, and dot with the remaining butter, broken into small pieces. Bake 40 minutes, until the top is crusty and slightly brown. Serve hot.

MUSSELS WITH TOMATOES, FENNEL, AND SAFFRON

S hellfish enjoy a special place in the galaxy of beloved ingredients in France, where the best mussels are found along the coast of Normandy. Mussels are a good shellfish for beginners, since they are so easily cleaned and steamed open. Here they are combined with typical flavors of the south of France. ✖ *Serves 4*

2 pounds (about 50) mussels
¼ cup olive oil
4 garlic cloves, peeled and minced
½ small fennel bulb, diced to make
   ½ cup
1½ cups dry white wine

1 tomato, peeled, seeded, and
   diced, or 2 canned peeled
   tomatoes
Generous pinch saffron, crushed
1 tablespoon chopped fresh basil
Salt

1] To clean the mussels if they have been farm-raised, simply rinse under cold water. Or, if they need more extensive cleaning, tug off the beards by hand and brush the shells under cold running water to remove any surface grit or debris. Reserve the mussels in a large mixing bowl, covered with a damp towel, in the refrigerator.

2] In a large stockpot or pasta pot, heat the olive oil over medium-low heat. Cook the garlic and fennel, stirring occasionally, until they begin to soften, about 5 minutes. Pour in the wine, tomatoes, and saffron and bring to a boil. Cook, uncovered, 5 minutes, to reduce the liquid and concentrate the flavors.

3] Add the mussels, cover the pot, and reduce the heat to medium. Cook, shaking occasionally to distribute the ingredients evenly, 7 minutes. Add the basil, cover, cook another minute, and remove from heat. Taste the broth and add salt as needed. Remove and discard any unopened mussels.

4] To serve, spoon a dozen or so mussels into each of 4 serving bowls. Ladle the broth over the top and serve hot with warm, crusty bread.

SCALLOPS
BEURRE BLANC

Fine satiny beurre blanc sauce is the classic accompaniment for fish. Most people love it—until you tell them how much butter they are eating! Serve over a bed of white rice to offset the richness. ✕ *Serves 4*

2 pounds sea or bay scallops
Salt
Freshly ground black pepper
12 tablespoons (1½ sticks) cold
   unsalted butter
2 shallots, minced

½ cup dry white wine
2 tablespoons heavy cream
3 tablespoons chopped fresh
   tarragon
Juice of ½ lemon

1] Wash and dry the scallops. If using small bay scallops leave whole. Slice sea scallops in half across the width. Sprinkle all over with salt and pepper.

2] Melt a tablespoon of the butter in a large skillet over high heat. Sauté the scallops about 2 minutes, stirring and tossing to sear evenly. Transfer to a platter and pour off any liquid in the pan.

3] Combine the shallots and white wine in the same skillet and cook over high heat until only a small pool of liquid remains in the pan, about 5 minutes.

4] Pour in the cream and continue boiling rapidly until it is reduced by half. Then reduce the heat to low. Cut the cold butter into tablespoon-sized pieces. Add the butter, 1 slice at a time, stirring constantly with a wooden spoon. As soon as one slice has melted, stir in the next, until they are all incorporated. Quickly stir in the tarragon and lemon juice and turn off the heat. Return the scallops to the pan, toss with the sauce, and then spoon onto serving plates.

INAUTHENTIC
BOUILLABAISSE

Jean-François Meteigner, the former chef at L'Orangerie, one of the most celebrated French restaurants in Los Angeles, devised this method of making the famous fish stew of Marseilles in about 30 minutes. The traditional accompaniments are toasted croutons spread with aioli, the garlic mayonnaise on page 33. Other white fish fillets such as sole, flounder, orange roughy, or halibut may be substituted, according to what is in the market. ✒ *Serves 4*

¼ cup olive oil
6 large garlic cloves, peeled and
    minced
1 large onion, peeled and chopped
3 tomatoes, seeded and diced
3 cups fish stock, or half bottled
    clam juice and half water
½ teaspoon (a small vial) saffron
    threads, chopped
3 sprigs thyme

1 teaspoon salt
¼ teaspoon cayenne
1 pound monkfish fillets, cut in
    1½- by 1-inch chunks
1 pound sea bass fillets, cut in
    1½- by 1-inch chunks
1 pound red snapper fillets, cut in
    1½- by 1-inch chunks
½ pound medium shrimp, in the
    shell

1] In a large nonaluminum stockpot or dutch oven, heat the olive oil over medium-high heat. Sauté the garlic and onion until soft, about 7 minutes. Then stir in the tomatoes, reduce the heat slightly, and cook another 5 minutes.

2] Pour in the fish stock or clam juice and water combination, add the saffron, thyme, salt, and cayenne, and bring to a boil over high heat.

3] Add the monkfish and cook 2 minutes. Then stir in the sea bass, reduce the heat to medium high, and cook 2 more minutes. Add the red snapper and shrimp (in the shell) and cook about 2 minutes longer, until all the fish is cooked through but not flaking apart. Ladle into bowls and serve hot.

SALMON ON A BED OF LENTILS

In this contemporary bistro dish, earthy lentils and light, fresh tomatoes provide the contrast and fullness traditionally provided by a sauce. This is a good dish for entertaining, because the lentils and tomatoes can be prepared in advance and brought back to temperature while the fish is being cooked. ✕ *Serves 4*

1½ cups green lentils
2 tablespoons unsalted butter
2 leeks, white part only, cleaned and diced
1 carrot, peeled and diced
3 garlic cloves, peeled and minced
1¾ cups fish stock or water
1 bay leaf
Salt

Freshly ground black pepper
3 Italian plum tomatoes, roughly chopped
3 tablespoons olive oil
3 fresh basil leaves, chopped
1½ pounds center-cut salmon fillet, cut into 4 pieces across the width

1] Place the lentils in a strainer and rinse in cold running water.

2] Melt 1 tablespoon of the butter in a medium pot over medium-high heat. Sauté the leeks, carrots, and 2 of the minced garlic cloves until golden, about 5 minutes. Then add the lentils, fish stock or water, and bay leaf. Bring to a boil, reduce to a simmer, and cook, covered, about 25 to 35 minutes. (The lentils should be cooked through and the liquid completely absorbed when done.) Remove and discard the bay leaf. Season to taste with salt and pepper and reserve with the cover on.

3] While the lentils are cooking, combine the tomatoes, 2 tablespoons of the olive oil, the basil, and the remaining minced garlic in a small bowl. Season with salt and pepper, mix, and set aside at room temperature.

4] When the lentils are done, cook the fish. Melt the remaining tablespoon each of butter and oil in a large skillet over high heat. Season the fish all over with salt and pepper. Sauté until browned on the outside and rare inside, about 2 minutes per side.

5] To serve, divide the lentils into 4 portions and spread a layer on each serving plate. Top each with a piece of salmon and then spoon the chopped tomato mixture over the fish. Serve hot.

SEA BASS WITH FENNEL AND TOMATO BUTTER SAUCE

Licorice-scented fennel, marinated ripe tomatoes, and fresh herbs frame sea bass in this elegant Provençal fish dish. ✖ *Serves 4*

1 tablespoon olive oil
2 large fennel bulbs, cut in half and thinly sliced
Salt
4 tablespoons (½ stick) unsalted butter
2 tomatoes, peeled, seeded, and diced

2 teaspoons chopped fresh Italian parsley
2 teaspoons chopped fresh tarragon
Freshly ground black pepper
2 pounds skinless, boneless sea bass
Olive oil

1] Preheat the grill or broiler.

2] Heat the olive oil in a medium skillet over medium-high heat. Turn the heat to low and add the fennel and ¼ teaspoon salt. Cover the pan and cook, stirring occasionally, until soft, about 20 minutes. Reserve with the cover on.

3] Meanwhile melt the butter in a small saucepan over medium-low heat. Stir in the tomatoes, parsley, tarragon, salt, and pepper and cook just until blended, about 3 minutes. Transfer to a food processor or blender and purée.

4] Rub the fish with olive oil and sprinkle with salt and pepper. Rub the grill grate or broiler tray with oil. Grill the fish about 3 minutes per side. Divide into 4 servings.

5] To serve, divide the fennel into 4 portions and place in the center of 4 serving plates. Top each bed of fennel with a portion of fish and spoon on the puréed tomato mixture. Serve immediately.

SEARED TUNA
SALAD NIÇOISE

First there was the real tuna Niçoise—canned oil-packed tuna, hard-boiled eggs, plenty of anchovies, and no potatoes—and then came all the variations. This one, featuring seared fresh tuna coated with garlic, makes a substantial main-course salad. ✗ *Serves 4*

¼ pound green beans, preferably French
1 pound red baby new potatoes, washed
1 medium head romaine lettuce, washed and dried
1 medium head red oak leaf lettuce, washed and dried
2 anchovies
1 teaspoon capers

¼ cup lemon juice
½ cup plus 1 tablespoon extra virgin olive oil
¼ teaspoon cracked black pepper
¼ teaspoon salt
1 pound tuna fillet
Salt
2 tablespoons puréed garlic
½ cup Niçoise olives

1] Bring salted water to a boil in a medium saucepan. If you are using French beans, leave them untrimmed and whole. For American beans, trim and cut into ½-inch lengths. Cook in boiling water for 2 minutes, drain, and transfer to a bowl of cold water to stop the cooking. Set aside to dry on paper towels.

2] Fill the saucepan with water again and bring to a boil. Add a pinch of salt and the potatoes and cook about 20 minutes. Drain, rinse with cold water, and set aside to dry on paper towels.

3] Cut or break the salad greens into bite-sized pieces and place in a mixing bowl. Reserve in the refrigerator.

4] To make the dressing, combine the anchovies, capers, lemon juice, ½ cup of the olive oil, pepper, and salt in a blender. Purée until the anchovies are in small chunks, about 2 minutes. Set aside.

5] Cut the tuna lengthwise into strips about 1 inch wide. Sprinkle all over with salt and then coat with the puréed garlic.

6] Heat a large skillet over high heat and coat with the remaining tablespoon of oil. Cook the tuna about 2 minutes per side and then transfer to a cutting board and let rest.

7] Meanwhile toss the salad with about half of the reserved salad dressing. Arrange on 4 dinner plates. Cut the tuna across the width into

½-inch slices and fan over each salad. Divide the green beans, potatoes, and olives and arrange around the rims of each plate. Drizzle the remaining dressing over the potatoes, beans, and fish, and serve.

VARIATION: For purists, substitute 1 small can of imported tuna packed in olive oil per person. Do not drain the tuna. Simply turn out of the can, flake, and arrange in the center of each bed of lettuce. Dress as for the fresh tuna.

PAN-FRIED TROUT WITH CAPERS, LEMON, AND PARSLEY

Like most fish, trout tastes best cooked quickly and cleanly, as it is in this classic preparation also known as trout meunière. ✖ *Serves 2*

Two 8-ounce whole trout, heads
   and tails left on, cleaned
Salt
Freshly ground black pepper
¼ cup all-purpose flour
1 tablespoon olive oil

4 tablespoons (½ stick) unsalted
   butter
1½ teaspoons capers
2 tablespoons chopped fresh
   Italian parsley
Juice of 1 lemon

1] Wash and dry the fish and sprinkle all over with salt and pepper. Scatter the flour on a platter and dip the fish to coat all over, patting off any excess flour.

2] Preheat the oven to 250 F.

3] In a skillet, heat the oil and 1 tablespoon of the butter over medium-high heat. When the pan is hot, add the fish and fry about 3 minutes per side. To prevent sticking, lift the fish occasionally with a spatula and shift its position in the pan. Reduce the heat slightly if the fat starts smoking. Transfer the fish to an ovenproof platter and keep warm in the oven.

4] Wipe the bottom of the skillet clean with several layers of paper towels and return to the stove. Melt the remaining butter over low heat. Swirl in the capers, parsley, and lemon juice and cook a minute or two. Spoon the sauce over the fish and serve hot.

PEPPERED SWORDFISH
WITH OLIVES AND LEMON

Swordfish, which can be used interchangeably with fresh tuna, stands up well to the strong flavors of cracked pepper, black olives, and lemon in this tasty 15-minute entrée. Serve with Cold Tomato and Cucumber Soup (page 27), and some boiled new potatoes for an elegant summer dinner. ✂ *Serves 4*

4 swordfish steaks
Coarse salt
1 tablespoon plus 1 teaspoon
cracked black pepper
⅓ cup plus 2 tablespoons extra
virgin olive oil

¼ cup Kalamata olives, sliced off
the pit and roughly chopped
½ teaspoon grated lemon zest

1] Wash the fish and pat dry. Lightly sprinkle all over with salt. Divide the cracked black pepper into 4 parts and generously coat both sides of each piece with pepper.

2] Preheat the oven to 200 F.

3] Heat 1 tablespoon of the olive oil in a large skillet over highest heat. Sear the fish, 2 pieces at a time, 2 minutes per side, adding a tablespoon of oil between batches. Transfer the first 2 pieces to an oven-proof platter and keep warm in the oven. Sear the remaining pieces of fish.

4] While the second batch is cooking, place a small skillet or saucepan over medium-high heat and pour in the remaining ⅓ cup of olive oil. Add the olives and lemon zest and cook, swirling the pan frequently, just to heat and release the flavors, less than a minute. Pour the hot oil over the fish and serve at once.

VEGETABLE SIDE DISHES

IF YOU HAVE EVER SEEN THE CARE AND CONCENTRATION BROUGHT TO BEAR ON SELECTING FRESH PRODUCE AT A FRENCH MARKET, YOU KNOW THAT THE FRENCH BRING AS MUCH PASSION TO THE PREPARATION OF THEIR VEGETABLES AS THEY DO TO A FILET MIGNON. THE PHILOSOPHY IS CONSISTENT. START WITH THE FINEST INGREDIENTS AND ACCENTUATE THEIR NATURAL GOODNESS. IN THIS ABUNDANT FARMING COUNTRY, PLEBEIAN POTATOES AND LEEKS GET AS MUCH RESPECT AS THEIR MORE SOPHISTICATED RELATIONS, THE ELEGANT ASPARAGUS AND ARTICHOKE.

MASHED POTATOES
WITH ROASTED GARLIC

The French have such a fetish for mashed potatoes that Joel Robuchon of Jamin—one of the best-known contemporary restaurants in Paris—built his reputation in part on the strength of his potato purée. The version presented here is for garlic and potato lovers only.

Serves 4

2 to 2½ pounds baking potatoes, such as Idahos, peeled and quartered
1 tablespoon salt
8 heads Roasted Garlic (page 80)
4 tablespoons (½ stick) unsalted butter, in tablespoon-sized pieces

½ cup milk
2 tablespoons extra virgin olive oil
Salt
Freshly ground black pepper

1] Place the potatoes in a medium saucepan and cover generously with water. Bring to a boil and add the salt. Reduce to a simmer and cook, uncovered, until the potatoes slip off a fork, about 15 minutes.

2] Meanwhile combine the roasted mashed garlic, the butter, and milk in a small pan. Cook over low heat, stirring occasionally, until the butter is melted and smooth.

3] When the potatoes are ready, drain them by holding the cover loosely over the top of the pot and pouring off the water. Mash the potatoes in the pot with a potato masher or fork.

4] Place the potatoes over low heat and mash in the garlic mixture until well combined. Then, with a wooden spoon, stir in the olive oil. (This is a chunky purée.) Season generously with salt and pepper and serve hot.

POTATO GRATIN

When it becomes necessary to abandon your low-cholesterol cooking for something a bit more soul-satisfying, what could be better than a classic potato gratin? Brown and crusty on the outside, mild, rich, and creamy inside, every calorie is guaranteed to bring pure pleasure. Potato gratin can be made in advance and reheated. ✖ *Serves 4*

Butter	¾ teaspoon salt
3 garlic cloves	Freshly ground black pepper
4 large baking potatoes, peeled	¼ teaspoon ground nutmeg
1 cup heavy cream	1 cup grated Gruyère cheese

1] Preheat oven to 350 F. Coat a 9- by 13-inch glass or ceramic roasting or lasagne pan with butter. Peal and crush a garlic clove and rub the inside of the pan. Peel and mince the other 2 garlic cloves and reserve.

2] Thinly slice the potatoes across the width in a food processor fitted with the 4-mm blade, or by hand. Evenly layer the potato slices in the prepared pan.

3] Bring the cream to a boil in a small saucepan. Pour over the potatoes. Spinkle with the minced garlic, salt, pepper, and nutmeg. Top with the grated cheese. Bake, uncovered, about 1 hour, or until the top is golden brown and the cream bubbly. Serve hot.

WARM POTATO SALAD WITH PARSLEY VINAIGRETTE

This traditional French potato salad cooks quickly and is an excellent choice for picnics and potluck meals. ✖ *Serves 6*

2½ pounds white or red boiling potatoes, unpeeled	Freshly ground black pepper
2 tablespoons red wine vinegar	½ cup olive oil
1 tablespoon lemon juice	1 cup (about 10) chopped shallots
2 teaspoons Dijon mustard	¼ cup chopped fresh Italian parsley
½ teaspoon salt	2 tablespoons capers

1] Wash the potatoes and slice them thinly across the width, using the 2-mm blade of the food processor. Transfer to a large bowl. Remove excess starch by filling the bowl with cold water and then pouring off the milky water about 3 times until water runs clear.

2] In a small bowl, whisk together the red wine vinegar, lemon juice, mustard, salt, pepper, and olive oil to make a dressing.

3] Meanwhile bring a large pot of salted water to a boil. Add the potatoes, let the water return to a boil and cook 1 minute. Drain in a colander and immediately transfer to a large mixing bowl. (Do not rinse.) Toss with the shallots.

4] Pour on the vinaigrette, parsley, and capers and mix well. Serve hot, at room temperature, or cold. Potato salad keeps in a sealed container in the refrigerator up to 3 days.

MATCHSTICK POTATOES

My eleven-year-old's favorite French food—shoestring french fries! Make sure you use the high burning point oils called for in the recipe in order to avoid smoking oil and burnt potatoes. ✕ *Serves 4*

2 quarts peanut or corn oil
4 baking potatoes (about 2½
    pounds)

Salt

1] Heat the oil in a stockpot or large saucepan over high heat to deep-fry temperature, 350 F. (This takes about 15 minutes.)

2] Meanwhile, wash and peel the potatoes. Use the 6-mm julienne blade in the food processor, or any other slicer you may have, to cut the potatoes into matchsticks. Place in a large bowl and rinse under cold running water until the water runs clear to remove surface starch. Drain and pat thoroughly dry with paper towels. (This step is important to prevent oil from splattering.)

3] If you do not have a thermometer, test the oil by dropping one piece of potato into it. If bubbles form immediately and it rises to the surface, the oil is ready. Standing back from the stovetop, add the potatoes, a handful at a time, and fry until pale golden and crisp, about 5 minutes a batch. Remove with slotted spoons or a strainer and drain on paper towels. Sprinkle with salt and serve.

ROASTED GARLIC

Roasted garlic develops a sweet, mellow, almost nutty flavor and buttery consistency. It makes an excellent spread for croutons.

✖ Serves 4 as an appetizer; makes ¼ cup roasted garlic purée

4 medium heads garlic, unpeeled   Olive oil
  and tops sliced

1] Preheat the oven to 500 F. Lightly coat a small roasting pan with olive oil.

2] Stand the garlic heads in the pan. Drizzle with olive oil and bake, uncovered, until blackened in spots and softened, 25 minutes. Transfer to small plates and serve with toasted bread for spreading.

3] To make purée, set garlic aside to cool about 20 minutes and then separate the cloves and release the roasted garlic by lightly pressing the cloves between your fingers. Mash with the tines of a fork.

TOMATOES PROVENÇAL

Baked tomatoes with a crisp topping of bread crumbs and herbs are a standard Provençal accompaniment to grilled and roasted meats and fish. Feel free to substitute other herbs, such as chives, chervil, or tarragon, according to taste and availability. ✖ *Serves 4*

4 large ripe tomatoes
4 garlic cloves, peeled and minced
1 tablespoon chopped fresh basil
1 tablespoon chopped fresh Italian
  parsley

6 tablespoons dry bread crumbs
3 tablespoons olive oil, plus extra
  for drizzling
½ teaspoon salt
Freshly ground black pepper

1] Preheat the oven to 425 F.

2] Wash and dry the tomatoes. Remove the stems and cut tomatoes in half through the width. Place cut side up on a baking tray or in an ovenproof casserole.

3] In a small bowl, make a paste by combining the garlic, fresh herbs, bread crumbs, olive oil, salt, and pepper. Spread about a tablespoon of the paste over each tomato half and drizzle with olive oil. Bake 30 minutes. Serve hot or at room temperature.

BRAISED LEEKS

Leeks, a mild-mannered cousin of the onion, take on a sweet homey quality in this simple braised side dish. ✖ *Serves 4*

3 pounds leeks (about 5 large)	¼ teaspoon ground white pepper
3 tablespoons unsalted butter	½ cup dry white wine
3 garlic cloves, peeled and minced	1 cup chicken stock
1 teaspoon salt	½ teaspoon fresh chopped thyme

1] Trim off the root ends and the dark green parts of leeks. Cut in half lengthwise and then rinse under cold running water to remove sand between layers. Cut each half lengthwise into 4 strips.

2] Melt 2 tablespoons butter in a large skillet over medium heat. Sauté the leeks and garlic with salt and pepper until they begin to soften, about 8 minutes. Pour in the wine, turn up the heat, and cook until the wine is nearly all absorbed. Then add the chicken stock, reduce the heat to low, cover, and cook 25 minutes. Stir in the thyme and the remaining tablespoon butter. Taste for salt and pepper and serve.

ZUCCHINI AND
TOMATO TIAN

Zucchinis and tomatoes are one of the great natural combinations of the summer garden. This easy casserole goes well with fish, poultry, or lamb. ✗ *Serves 6*

¼ cup olive oil
1½ pounds (about 4) ripe tomatoes, stemmed
1½ pounds (about 4) medium zucchinis, ends trimmed

Salt
Freshly ground black pepper
2 garlic cloves, peeled and minced
1 tablespoon chopped fresh thyme, basil, or parsley

1] Preheat the oven to 350 F. Coat a 9- by 12-inch ovenproof baking dish or lasagne pan with olive oil.

2] Cut the tomatoes and zucchinis across the width into ¼-inch slices.

3] Arrange half of the zucchini slices over the bottom of the pan. Cover with half of the tomatoes, sprinkle with salt and pepper, and drizzle lightly with olive oil. Repeat a layer of zucchinis and then tomatoes. Sprinkle with garlic, fresh herbs, salt, pepper, and olive oil. Bake 1¼ hours. Serve hot or at room temperature.

ASPARAGUS

You know people take a vegetable seriously when they develop a special plate on which to serve it. I think this most delicate of green vegetables tastes best eaten simply, with plain butter or vinaigrette rather than a heavy sauce, although a recipe for hollandaise sauce is given on page 100. In France, asparagus is often served as a first course.

✗ Serves 4

1 pound asparagus
½ teaspoon salt
4 tablespoons (½ stick) unsalted
  butter

Salt
Freshly ground black pepper

1] Rinse the asparagus and remove the woody ends by bending the stalks and letting them snap where they naturally break. It is not necessary to peel thin asparagus. Thick stalks should be peeled with a paring knife up to about an inch from the tip.

2] Fill a large skillet with about an inch of water and bring to a boil. Add the salt, reduce to a simmer, and add the asparagus. Cook, uncovered, 5 to 10 minutes, depending on size. Drain and pat dry with paper towels.

3] To serve hot, you can merely transfer to a serving dish, top with pats of butter, and season to taste with salt and pepper. Or for a slightly nutty flavor, you can make browned butter by melting the butter in a small light-colored saucepan or skillet over medium heat until small brown particles begin to form. Pour over hot asparagus, and serve with salt and pepper.

4] To serve cold, rinse the drained asparagus in cold water to stop the cooking and then dry with paper towels. Chill and serve with a Classic Vinaigrette (page 99) or garlic mayonnaise (see Aioli, page 33).

RATATOUILLE

I prefer my mélange of Provençal vegetables the old-fashioned way—moist and stewy like a chutney, with not an al dente vegetable in sight. A great dish to keep on hand for summer entertaining, ratatouille can be served warm or cold, as a vegetable side dish or as an appetizer with slices of grilled Italian or French bread. Japanese eggplant does not need to be presalted, since these smaller eggplants have fewer seeds to give off moisture. ✖ *Serves 6 to 8*

½ cup olive oil
2 large onions, peeled and chopped
8 garlic cloves, peeled and minced
1 teaspoon salt
½ teaspoon freshly ground black pepper
¼ teaspoon red pepper flakes
2 red bell peppers, cored, seeded, and cut into ½-inch squares
1 pound (about 4) Japanese eggplants
3 medium (4-ounce) zucchinis

¼ pound French green beans (optional), trimmed and cut in ½-inch lengths
One 28-ounce can Italian peeled tomatoes, drained, seeded, and roughly chopped
2 tablespoons chopped fresh basil
1 tablespoon chopped fresh thyme
½ teaspoon dried rosemary
2 bay leaves
Juice of ½ lemon

1] Heat ¼ cup of the olive oil in a large dutch oven or saucepan over medium heat. Sauté the onions and garlic, along with salt, pepper, and red pepper flakes, until the onions begin to soften, about 10 minutes. Add the red bell pepper and cook an additional 10 minutes, stirring frequently.

2] Meanwhile trim the eggplants and zucchinis and chop into ½-inch dice. Add to the pot along with the green beans and remaining olive oil. Turn up the heat, add the tomatoes and herbs, and bring nearly to a boil, stirring frequently.

3] Reduce to a simmer and cook, covered, until the vegetables are soft and the flavors blend, about 40 minutes. Stir in the lemon juice and remove from heat. Adjust seasonings with salt and pepper and serve hot, at room temperature, or chilled.

LENTIL SALAD

The key to this refreshing salad is to combine the vinaigrette and beans while the beans are still warm to better absorb the dressing. The tiny, dense, dark green lentils from Puy in central France are considered a delicacy and can be found in specialty shops in the United States.
✘ *Serves 4*

1 cup green lentils
¼ cup red wine vinegar
2 tablespoons freshly squeezed lemon juice
½ teaspoon Dijon mustard
½ teaspoon salt

½ teaspoon black pepper
½ cup olive oil
1 medium red onion, peeled and finely diced
1 tablespoon chopped fresh basil leaves

1] Pick out any stones and rinse the lentils. Place in a small saucepan and pour in enough cold water to cover generously. Bring to a boil, reduce to a simmer, and cook, uncovered, until soft but not mushy, 20 to 25 minutes.

2] While the beans simmer, whisk together the red wine vinegar, lemon juice, Dijon mustard, salt, pepper, and olive oil in a small bowl to form a dressing.

3] Strain the warm lentils and transfer to a bowl. Add the red onion and basil and pour on the dressing. Stir and toss to combine thoroughly. Serve warm, or chill. Lentil salad keeps in the refrigerator up to 2 days. Do not reheat, but bring to room temperature before serving.

BOILED ARTICHOKES

What could be more French than plain boiled artichokes with melted butter or mayonnaise? One Frenchman I know keeps his refrigerator stocked with them, boiled and ready for snacking.

Artichokes
1 tablespoon salt

Juice of 1 lemon

1] Wash the artichokes and trim off each stem so the base is flat. Pull off and discard the bottom row or two of leaves. It is not necessary to snip off the pointy ends with scissors unless you prefer to do so.

2] Bring a large stockpot or saucepan of water to a rolling boil. Add the artichokes, salt, and lemon juice. Cook at a simmer, uncovered, 45 minutes. Drain upside down in a colander so water doesn't remain in the leaves, and serve hot with melted butter, Classic Vinaigrette (page 99), Hollandaise Sauce (page 100), or Homemade Mayonnaise (page 100). Artichokes are also delicious eaten cold with the same sauces or just sprinkled with salt and pepper.

WILD MUSHROOMS PROVENÇAL

Simple and heavenly—mushrooms cooked quickly with garlic and parsley. ✖ *Serves 4*

1 pound fresh wild mushrooms
   such as chanterelles, shiitakes,
   or oysters
¼ cup olive oil
3 garlic cloves, peeled and minced

2 tablespoons chopped fresh Italian
   parsley
Juice of ½ lemon
Salt
Freshly ground black pepper

1] Wipe the mushrooms clean with damp paper towels. Trim the stem ends and roughly chop the mushrooms into large chunks.

2] Heat the oil in a large skillet over medium-high heat. Sauté the garlic a minute or two just to release the aroma, and add the mushrooms. Sauté, stirring and tossing frequently, until the oil is absorbed and the mushrooms are glossy, about 2 minutes. Stir in the parsley and lemon juice, season with salt and pepper, and serve hot.

DESSERTS

When the French entertain at home, it is not unusual for them to bring in a cake from the local patisserie, or simply to serve fresh fruit and cheese, rather than attempt making an elaborate restaurant-style dessert themselves. On that practical note, all of the desserts collected here are unfussy home-style ones that deliver maximum pleasure for minimum toil. Coffee, in the French style, is traditionally taken black following dessert, and when there is a cheese tray, it is brought out before dessert.

CHOCOLATE ESPRESSO MOUSSE

It is worth splurging on a high-quality chocolate like Tobler, Lindt, or Callebaut when making such a pure chocolate dessert. ✖ *Serves 6*

5 ounces bittersweet chocolate, roughly chopped
2 tablespoons unsalted butter
1 tablespoon sugar
4 eggs

2 tablespoons strong cold coffee
Pinch of salt
Fresh berries, chocolate covered espresso beans, or Crème Chantilly (page 102) for garnish

1] Place the chopped chocolate, butter, and sugar in a heavy medium saucepan over low heat. Cook, stirring frequently, until the chocolate is melted and the mixture is smooth. Remove from heat.

2] Place 2 mixing bowls on the counter for separating the eggs. Working over the bowl for collecting the whites (the bowl must be perfectly clean and dry for the whites to rise properly), crack the eggs and collect the whites in one bowl and the yolks in the other.

3] With an electric beater, beat the yolks until pale and smooth. In order to heat the eggs gradually, spoon about ¼ of the chocolate mixture into the yolks and beat to combine. Then add the rest of the chocolate and mix at medium speed until well combined. Mix in the coffee.

4] Whisk the egg whites with salt until stiff, glossy peaks form. (If you are using an electric mixer, begin at low speed and gradually move to high.) Gently fold whites into the chocolate mixture, a third at a time, until no trace of the whites is visible.

5] Spoon into 6 small ramekins, custard cups, or aperitif glasses. Cover with plastic wrap and chill at least 4 hours, or preferably overnight. Garnish as desired and serve cold.

COLD PEACH AND
STRAWBERRY COMPOTE

The French have many easy, elegant ways to serve fresh fruit. This one makes a great refreshing dessert for a hot summer night. ✖ *Serves 6*

2 pints ripe strawberries
3 ripe medium peaches, washed
    and dried
2 tablespoons sugar

2 tablespoons Grand Marnier or
    other orange liqueur
¼ cup fresh orange juice

1] Wash and dry the strawberries and remove the stems. Cut half of the berries lengthwise into quarters and place in a medium bowl.

2] Cut the peaches in half, removing the pits. Then cut each half into 4 slices, and each slice into thirds. (The strawberry and peach pieces should be about the same size.) Add the peaches to the bowl with strawberries and gently toss.

3] Cut the remaining berries in half and place in the bowl of a food processor fitted with the metal blade. Add the sugar, Grand Marnier, and orange juice. Process until a smooth sauce is formed. Pour over the fruit in the bowl. Stir and toss to combine, cover with plastic wrap, and chill at least 6 hours or as long as 2 days. Serve cold.

STRAWBERRY ALMOND
TART

Once you master sweet tart dough or pâte sucrée in the food processor, you may have a difficult time serving anything but fruit tarts to honored guests. They are so beautiful and well loved.

This easy almond cream filling, known as frangipane, is one of the classic bases for fruit and berry tarts. It is also delicious with apricots, plums, or pears baked into the cream. ✖ *Serves 6 to 8*

1 recipe Pâte Sucrée (page 108)

ALMOND CREAM FILLING————
6 tablespoons sugar
½ cup slivered blanched almonds
6 tablespoons (¾ stick) unsalted
  butter, softened

1 egg
1 egg yolk
1 tablespoon brandy
½ teaspoon vanilla extract
Pinch of salt
1½ pints ripe strawberries

1] Line a 10-inch tart shell with pâte sucrée and refrigerate 30 minutes. Preheat the oven to 425 F.

2] To make the almond filling, combine the sugar and almonds in a food processor and process with the metal blade until the nuts are finely ground. Add the butter, a tablespoon at a time, processing well after each addition. Add the egg, egg yolk, brandy, vanilla, and salt and continue processing until a smooth, liquidy paste is formed. Set aside. (If making in advance, reserve in a sealed container in the refrigerator for up to a week. Return to room temperature before using.)

3] Prick the pastry on the bottom of the tart shell about 6 times with the tines of a fork to prevent shrinkage and then bake 12 minutes. Set aside on a counter to rest for 5 minutes and reduce the heat in the oven to 375 F. (Don't be worried about the dough puffing. It will deflate in a minute or two.) Pour the almond paste into the tart shell and return it to the oven. Bake until the top is golden brown, about 25 minutes. Set on a rack to cool for 1 hour.

4] Gently wash the strawberries and pat dry. Working with the point of a paring knife, remove the stems by cutting out cones in the top of the berries. Then cut in half lengthwise. Beginning at the outside edge of the tart shell, arrange the berries cut sides down in a circular pattern so that the bottom tips fit into the little **V**s at the top of each berry. Reserve one small, perfect berry to place in the center. Refrigerate until serving time.

VARIATIONS: To substitute apricots or plums for the berries, bake the almond paste in the pastry shell for 10 minutes and remove. Top with the halved, pitted fruits. Return to the oven and bake 20 to 30 minutes more, until the fruit is soft and the paste golden. Pears may be added at the same time, but peel, core, and slice them first and arrange the fanned slices over the partially cooked almond paste.

TARTE TATIN

Of the many wonderful apple desserts in the traditional French repertoire, this caramelized upside down apple tart is probably the best known. This version, adapted from the Ma Cuisine Cooking School in Los Angeles, eliminates the need for a special pan. It can be cooked entirely in an ovenproof skillet. Sheets of Pepperidge Farm frozen puff pastry can be found in the frozen pastry section of the supermarket.
✖ *Serves 6 to 8*

3½ pounds (about 14) small Red Delicious apples
8 tablespoons (1 stick) unsalted butter

¾ cup sugar
1 sheet (½ pound) frozen puff pastry

1] Cut the apples into quarters. Peel, core, and place in a bowl.

2] Combine the butter and sugar in a 10-inch sauté pan with ovenproof handle. Cook over medium heat, stirring occasionally, until the butter melts and the mixture is smooth and yellow. Remove from heat.

3] Over the butter mixture in the pan, arrange a layer of apples in a spiral pattern. Continue piling on the apples, filling in the spaces, until all are used. Do not be concerned if the pan is overcrowded—the apples will shrink as they cook.

4] Return pan to heat and cook without stirring, uncovered, over medium-low heat for 1 hour 20 minutes, or until the liquid in the pan is brown and bubbly and smells of caramel. Set aside to cool 10 minutes.

5] While the apples are cooking, preheat the oven to 375 F. Defrost the frozen pastry about 20 minutes, or follow the instructions on the package.

6] Roll out the pastry on a lightly floured board with a floured rolling pin to a 12-inch circle. (If you are using square sheets, just trim off the corners with a sharp blade.) Prick all over with a fork and place on a platter in the refrigerator. (The trick to working with puff pastry is to handle it as little as possible and to keep it cold.)

7] When the apples are done, place the cold pastry over the top of the pan, tucking in any excess dough. Place in the oven and bake until the pastry is well puffed and golden, 30 minutes. Set aside to cool 20 minutes. To serve, place a large flat serving platter over the pan, quickly invert, and lift off the pan. Rearrange the apples to even out the top and spoon any extra caramel sauce over all. Serve warm with whipped cream or vanilla ice cream.

PEAR ANISE
CRÈME BRULÉE

A thin layer of puréed pears and the scent of anise add an interesting twist to this rich custard with crisp sugar crust—a lovely dessert to serve in the fall or winter when pears are at their peak. ✗ *Serves 6*

2 ripe pears, peeled, cored, and
    thinly sliced
½ cup plus 3½ tablespoons sugar
Juice of ½ lemon
2 cups heavy cream

One 2-inch length vanilla bean, or
    1 tablespoon vanilla extract
6 egg yolks
1 tablespoon Pernod or other anise-
    flavored liqueur

1] Combine the pears, ¼ cup water, and 1½ tablespoons of the sugar in a small saucepan. Bring to a boil, reduce to a simmer, and cook until the pears fall apart when pressed with a wooden spoon, about 20 minutes. Add the lemon juice and transfer to a food processor or blender to purée. Set aside.

2] Pour the cream into a heavy medium saucepan. Split open the vanilla bean with a paring knife and scrape the seeds into the cream; then add the bean. Bring just to a boil and remove from heat. Remove the bean.

3] In a mixing bowl, whisk together the egg yolks and ¼ cup of the sugar until smooth and pale yellow. Whisk in the vanilla extract, if using.

4] Slowly warm the eggs by whisking about ½ cup of the hot cream into the yolk mixture. Then pour that mixture into the pan with the cream. Cook over low heat, stirring constantly with a wooden spoon, until the mixture is thick enough to leave to trail when a finger is drawn across the spoon, 3 to 6 minutes. Remove from heat and stir in the Pernod or other liqueur.

5] Spread about 2 tablespoons of the pear purée in the bottom of each of six ½-cup ovenproof remekins or custard cups. Ladle the warm custard over all and set aside to cool about ½ hour. Then cover with plastic wrap and chill at least 4 hours or as long as 2 days.

6] Just before serving, preheat the broiler. Sprinkle each serving evenly with a tablespoon of sugar. Set the dishes on a baking tray and place under the broiler until the tops are golden brown but not black, 1 to 4 minutes. Carefully transfer the hot dishes to dessert plates or saucers and serve immediately.

CRANBERRY CLAFOUTIS

This adaptation of the traditional batter cake with unpitted cherries from Limousin comes from Linda Zimmerman—friend, pudding maven, and author of *Puddings, Custards and Flans.* It is an easy, homey dish to serve for weekend brunch, with some sweetened whipped cream on the side. ✖ *Serves 6 to 8*

2½ tablespoons unsalted butter
¾ cup all-purpose flour
3 large eggs
¾ cup plus 2 tablespoons sugar
1 cup milk

1 teaspoon vanilla extract
Pinch of salt
2 cups (8 ounces) dried cranberries
2 tablespoons Grand Marnier

1] Preheat the oven to 375 F. Melt the butter in the oven in a 9-inch Pyrex pie plate for about 5 minutes.

2] In a food processor fitted with the metal blade or in a blender, combine the flour, eggs, ¾ cup of the sugar, the milk, vanilla extract, and salt. Process until well mixed, pour into a bowl, and set aside to rest 10 minutes.

3] Meanwhile combine the cranberries and Grand Marnier in a small bowl to soak for 10 minutes. Stir into the batter just to combine.

4] When the butter is melted, tilt the pie plate to coat it completely. Pour in the batter and sprinkle the remaining 2 tablespoons of sugar evenly over the top. Bake until golden brown and puffy, 45 minutes. Set aside to cool for 10 minutes—the pudding will fall and crack a bit. Serve warm or at room temperature from the pan with Crème Chantilly (page 102) or vanilla ice cream.

LITTLE ALMOND CAKES

The batter for these moist little butter and nut cakes, similar in concept to the *financiers* sold in Parisian bake shops, can be put together in 15 minutes. They are wonderful to nibble with afternoon tea or coffee, or to serve for dessert with fruity ice cream or sorbet.

✖ *Makes 20 small cakes*

1 cup whole blanched almonds
1½ cups confectioners' sugar
½ cup cake flour
Pinch of salt

¾ cup (about 6) egg whites
12 tablespoons (1½ sticks) unsalted
   butter, melted

1] Heat the oven to 350 F. Generously butter a mini muffin pan.

2] Spread the almonds on a baking sheet and toast in the oven, shaking the pan occasionally, until golden, about 12 minutes. Turn the oven up to 450 F.

3] Transfer the nuts to a food processor fitted with the metal blade and process until finely ground. (Always stay nearby when grinding nuts, as they can quickly turn into nut butter if overprocessed.) Add 1¼ cups sugar, the flour, and salt. Process until the mixture is well blended and then transfer to a mixing bowl.

4] Pour the unbeaten egg whites into the nut mixture and stir to combine. Then stir in the melted butter until well blended. Ladle the batter into the buttered muffin cups until ⅔ full.

5] Bake 7 minutes. Reduce the heat to 400 F and bake 10 minutes longer. Turn the oven off and let the pan rest in the oven 5 minutes. The muffins will be golden around the edges with little peaks in the center. Remove from oven and set aside to cool in the pan 10 minutes. Invert to remove. When the cakes are totally cool, press the remaining confectioners' sugar through a sieve to sprinkle on the tops. Almond cakes keep well up to 4 days.

QUICK AND EASY DESSERTS

These quick preparations are ideal after you've worked all day but yearn to put something elegant on the table for dessert.

RASPBERRY COULIS

A coulis is a smooth fresh fruit or vegetable sauce. This one is particularly good over vanilla or chocolate ice cream and close to perfection with the vanilla ice cream and raspberry sorbet combination sold in the supermarket. ✕ *Makes 1 cup, enough for 8 servings*

One 6-ounce basket raspberries, or one 10-ounce bag frozen berries, thawed

2 tablespoons confectioners' sugar
1 tablespoon lemon juice

Combine the ingredients in a food processor fitted with the metal blade and purée until smooth. This keeps in a sealed container in the refrigerator for 3 days, or in the freezer for a month.

BERRIES IN CHAMPAGNE

✕ *Serves 4*

2 pints strawberries, washed and hulled
¼ cup sugar

2 tablespoons fresh lemon juice
1 bottle cold Champagne

Cut the strawberries in quarters lengthwise and combine in a bowl with sugar and lemon juice. Cover and chill 1 to 2 hours. Divide the berries and their juice into 4 glass dessert dishes or wine goblets. Slowly pour in the cold Champagne to cover well and serve immediately.

SAUCES, STOCKS, AND DOUGHS

THESE RECIPES FOR THE BASIC FRENCH SAUCES, STOCKS, AND DOUGHS FORM THE BUILDING BLOCKS FOR MOST EUROPEAN-STYLE COOKING. NONE OF THEM IS DIFFICULT TO MASTER, ESPECIALLY WITH THE HELP OF A FOOD PROCESSOR.

CLASSIC VINAIGRETTE

The general rule of thumb for salad dressings is one part vinegar to three parts oil. Be fairly conservative if you decide to add minced garlic or fresh herbs, since a little raw garlic goes a long way. *Makes ½ cup*

1 teaspoon Dijon mustard
2 tablespoons red wine vinegar
6 tablespoons olive oil
Salt
Freshly ground black pepper

Whisk the mustard and red wine vinegar together in a small bowl. Add the olive oil, whisking vigorously to combine. Season to taste with salt and pepper and whisk again. Pour over salad or keep in a sealed container in the refrigerator up to a week. Whisk or shake to recombine.

LEMON VINAIGRETTE

This tart dressing goes well with a salad of rich ingredients like avocado or seafood. *Makes ½ cup*

¼ cup freshly squeezed lemon juice
¼ cup extra virgin olive oil
Salt
Freshly ground black pepper

Whisk the lemon juice and olive oil together in a bowl. Season with salt and pepper and whisk again.

HOMEMADE
MAYONNAISE

In France, mayonnaise is used to bind other ingredients like potato and blanched vegetable salads, but it is also enjoyed as a cold sauce for hard-boiled eggs, cold fish, and chicken. Fresh mayonnaise is a real treat. If you haven't ever used your food processor for that purpose, you will be amazed at how easy it is to make. A tablespoon or so of chopped fresh herbs such as tarragon, parsley, or chives is a nice addition to fresh mayonnaise. If you haven't been convinced to make your own, try adding herbs and a squeeze of lemon juice to your favorite bottled brand. They work wonders! ✻ *Makes 2 cups*

2 egg yolks
2 tablespoons fresh lemon juice
1 tablespoon Dijon mustard
1 cup safflower or other mild
    vegetable oil

½ cup olive oil
½ teaspoon salt
¼ teaspoon white pepper

1] Combine the egg yolks, lemon juice, and mustard in the bowl of a food processor fitted with a metal blade or in a blender and process until combined, about 30 seconds.

2] With the machine running, drizzle the oils through the feed tube in a slow steady stream (the pin hole in the feed tube pusher is perfect for this). Add the salt and pepper and process briefly just to combine. Homemade mayonnaise may be kept in a sealed container in the refrigerator for up to a week. Do not freeze.

HOLLANDAISE SAUCE

Rich, smooth hollandaise is easy to make in the food processor. It is an essential part of eggs benedict and a classic accompaniment to hot asparagus or broccoli. Egg-based sauces like hollandaise and béarnaise cannot be reheated but can be kept warm in a thermos or coffee carafe for about 2 hours. ✻ *Makes ¾ cup*

French Cooking for Beginners

3 egg yolks
1 tablespoon fresh lemon juice
¼ teaspoon salt

¼ teaspoon white pepper
12 tablespoons (1½ sticks) unsalted
butter

1] Combine the egg yolks, 1 tablespoon water, lemon juice, salt, and pepper in the bowl of a food processor fitted with the metal blade.

2] Melt the butter in a small saucepan over medium-high heat. With a small ladle or soup spoon remove and discard the white foam that rises to the top. Remove from heat.

3] Process the egg yolk mixture a few seconds just to combine. Then, with the machine running, drizzle the hot butter through the hole in the feed tube pusher until incorporated.

BÉARNAISE SAUCE

Grilled or broiled steak and béarnaise sauce—my husband's idea of heaven. ✕ *Makes ¾ cup*

½ cup red wine vinegar
3 shallots, peeled and finely
chopped
12 tablespoons (1½ sticks) unsalted
butter
3 eggs yolks

¼ teaspoon salt
¼ teaspoon freshly ground black
pepper
1 tablespoon chopped fresh
tarragon
1 tablespoon lemon juice

1] Combine the red wine vinegar and shallots in a small skillet or saucepan. Bring to a boil over high heat and cook until a thin film of liquid remains on the bottom of the pan, about 4 minutes. Discard shallots and strain the reduced vinegar into the bowl of a food processor fitted with the metal blade.

2] Melt the butter in a small saucepan over medium-high heat. Remove from heat.

3] Add the egg yolks, salt, and pepper to the strained, cooled vinegar and process just to combine. Then, with the machine running, slowly drizzle in the hot butter.

4] Transfer sauce to a bowl, stir in the tarragon and lemon juice, adjust salt and pepper, and serve warm.

CRÈME ANGLAISE

Crème anglaise, or English cream, is the standard French dessert sauce. It can be flavored with coffee by infusing the milk with finely ground espresso, or with such liqueurs as Kahlúa or Grand Marnier by stirring them in at the end. It goes well with fruit or pastry and is the basic custard used for making ice cream. ✖ *Makes 1¼ cup*

1 cup whole milk
4 large egg yolks

½ cup sugar
¾ teaspoon vanilla extract

1] Pour the milk into a heavy saucepan and bring nearly to a boil.

2] Whisk together the egg yolks and sugar until smooth and pale yellow.

3] Ladle a few spoonfuls of the warm milk into the eggs and whisk to combine. Then pour the egg mixture into the milk in the pan. Cook over low heat, stirring constantly with a wooden spoon, until thick enough to coat the spoon, about 5 minutes. Remove from heat and stir 2 minutes longer to stop the cooking. Cover and chill until serving time. (If some fine lumps have formed, pass through a strainer before serving.)

CRÈME CHANTILLY

Crème chantilly is nothing more than sweetened whipped cream with a much more melodious name. A dollop on a slice of cake or seasonal berries always makes the occasion seem more festive. ✖ *Makes 2 cups*

1 cup cold heavy cream
2½ tablespoons confectioners'
   sugar

2 teaspoons brandy

1] Using the chilled balloon whisk of an electric mixer, whisk cream at low speed until it starts to thicken and then turn the speed up to high.

2] When the cream is thick enough to hold a shape, sprinkle in sugar and brandy and whisk briefly. Store in the refrigerator up to a day.

To make crème chantilly by hand, whisk vigorously with a large chilled wire whisk, incorporating as much air as possible by lifting the cream with the whisk and turning the bowl. Whisk in the sugar and brandy at the end and ask for help as needed.

TOMATO COULIS

This smooth, sweet, uncomplicated tomato sauce goes well with fish and vegetables as well as pasta. ✗ *Makes 1²/₃ cups*

3½ tablespoons unsalted butter
2 garlic cloves, peeled and minced
2 small carrots, peeled and roughly chopped
4 shallots, peeled and chopped to make about 6 tablespoons

2 pounds ripe tomatoes (about 6 medium), cored
1 teaspoon salt
Freshly ground black pepper
2 teaspoons chopped fresh chervil, parsley, basil, or thyme

1] Melt 2 tablespoons of the butter in a large heavy saucepan over medium-high heat. Cook the garlic, carrots, and shallots until soft, about 6 minutes.

2] Meanwhile cut the tomatoes in half across the width and squeeze out the seeds. Roughly chop.

3] Add tomatoes to the pan, reduce heat to low, and cook, uncovered, 20 minutes. Stir occasionally to avoid scorching.

4] Transfer mixture to a food processor fitted with the metal blade, or to a blender, and purée. Pour back into the pan and place over low heat. Break the remaining butter into about 6 pieces and stir it into the sauce until it melts. Stir in the fresh herbs and remove from heat. Serve hot.

STOCKS

There is something pure and virtuous about making stocks from scratch. However, when you haven't the time, I recommend the frozen product called Perfect Additions, available in health food and specialty markets—especially for sauce-making. The taste is much purer than canned stock, a factor that really makes a difference in a reduced sauce.

CHICKEN STOCK

If you only attempt one stock, this is the one to try since it is the most versatile. Besides making excellent chicken soup, it can be used for most sauces, for braising meats and vegetables, and for adding flavor to such grains as rice, and to couscous. �҂ *Makes 3 ½ quarts*

3½ pounds chicken bones, necks, backs, and feet
2 celery ribs, sliced
2 carrots, peeled and sliced
1 large onion, peeled and quartered

1 bunch parsley stems
2 bay leaves
7 sprigs thyme, or 1 teaspoon dried
½ teaspoon black peppercorns
1 teaspoon salt

1] Wash the chicken parts and combine in a large stockpot with the remaining ingredients. Pour in enough cold water to cover generously, about 1 gallon. Bring to a boil. With a ladle, skim and discard the foam that rises to the top. Reduce to a simmer and cook, uncovered, for 2 hours, checking the pot and skimming off the foam occasionally.

2] Let cool slightly, then strain into storage containers. Chicken stock may be stored in the refrigerator up to a week and in the freezer for several months. The layer of chicken fat that forms on the top should be skimmed off and discarded.

VEAL STOCK

Rich, dark veal stock forms the basis for the deeper sauces traditionally served with beef, veal, and lamb. The best time to set up a pot of veal bones is before bedtime, since it simmers for such a long time. You may need to order the bones in advance from your butcher. When you do, have them cracked so their valuable gelatin is released more easily. ✕ *Makes 2 quarts*

5 pounds veal bones, such as
  shanks and shoulders
2 onions, peeled and halved
2 carrots, peeled and cut into large
  chunks
2 celery ribs, roughly chopped

1 leek, white and green, cleaned
  and chopped
2 cups dry white wine
2 teaspoons dried thyme
1 teaspoon black peppercorns
1 teaspoon salt

1] Preheat the oven to 400 F.

2] Line a large baking sheet or roasting pan with aluminum foil. Arrange the bones, onions, and carrots on it in one layer. Bake, turning occasionally, until the bones and vegetables are browned, about 45 minutes.

3] Transfer bones and vegetables to a stockpot, discarding the grease in the pan, and add celery, leek, and wine. Bring to a boil and reduce by half. Pour in enough cold water to cover, about 1 gallon, and the seasonings. Bring to a boil, reduce to a simmer, and cook, uncovered, 8 to 10 hours. Let cool slightly.

4] Strain and discard the solids. Set stock aside to cool to room temperature. Store in the refrigerator up to a week or in the freezer for several months. Skim and discard any fat from the top before using.

FISH STOCK

A busy fish market should have plenty of excess heads, bones, and tails on hand for making stock. You may need to call in advance, however, since these trimmings may automatically be discarded or recycled. Avoid trimmings from oily fish like tuna or salmon, since they will be too fatty and strong for a neutral stock. ✖ *Makes 6 cups*

2 tablespoons unsalted butter
1 carrot, peeled and cut in 1-inch lengths
2 celery ribs, cut in 1-inch lengths
1 onion, peeled and cut in 8 wedges
2 pounds fish bones and heads

1½ cups dry white wine
Bouquet garni of 2 bay leaves, 6 parsley sprigs, 4 thyme sprigs, and ¼ teaspoon black peppercorns tied in a square of cheesecloth
½ teaspoon salt

1] Melt the butter in a large nonaluminum stockpot over medium-high heat. Sauté the carrot, celery, and onion until golden, about 5 minutes. Then add the fish bones and heads and sauté another 5 minutes, stirring occasionally for even browning.

2] Pour in the wine, turn the heat up to high, and boil 4 minutes to concentrate the flavors and cook off the alcohol. Add 2 quarts cold water, the bouquet garni, and salt. Bring to a boil, reduce to a simmer, and cook, uncovered, 45 minutes.

3] Let cool and then strain the liquid, discarding the solids. Store in the refrigerator up to 3 days, or freeze up to a month.

French Cooking for Beginners

PÂTE BRISÉE

This is the unsweetened tart dough used for savory tarts and quiches. It is one of the easiest doughs to handle—a good one for beginners.
Makes one 10-inch tart shell

1¼ cups all-purpose flour	7 tablespoons cold butter
Pinch of salt	3 tablespoons iced water

1] Combine the flour and salt in a food processor fitted with the metal blade. Cut the cold butter into about 10 slices and add to the flour. Process about 15 seconds until the mixture turns pale yellow, with a consistency like cornmeal.

2] Gradually add the water through the feed tube while processing with short pulses about 9 times. The dough should hold together when pressed between your fingers, but it should not whirl around on top of the blade.

3] Empty the dough onto a sheet of plastic wrap and press into a 6-inch disk. Wrap well with plastic and refrigerate at least ½ hour or as long as a day.

4] To roll out the dough, lightly spread some flour over a wooden board and also rub the rolling pin with flour. Remove the dough from its plastic wrapping and press it on the floured board with the palm of a hand to flatten. Start rolling from the center out, making quarter turns and lifting the dough intermittently to be sure it isn't sticking. Dust with flour occasionally if the dough is sticky. (If the dough has been refrigerated for long, it may be too hard to roll. Just let it warm on the counter about 30 minutes, or warm with your hands before beginning.)

5] Carefully lift the rolled dough and drape it over a 9- or 10-inch tart pan with removable bottom. Press the dough into the sides with your fingers and crimp the edges into the flutes of the pan. Run a rolling pin across the top to remove any excess dough. The tart shell is now ready to be baked or reserved in the refrigerator for 2 days or in the freezer for a month. To bake the empty shell in advance, follow instructions in step 6 of the Pâte Sucrée recipe (page 108).

PÂTE SUCRÉE

This is the basic sweet dough for fruit tarts and cookies. ✖ *Makes one 10-inch tart shell*

1 cup all-purpose flour
Pinch of salt
2 tablespoons sugar
8 tablespoons (1 stick) cold unsalted
    butter

1 egg yolk
1½ tablespoons cold water

1] Place the flour, salt, and sugar in the bowl of a food processor fitted with the metal blade. Slice the cold butter into about 12 pieces and add to the flour. Pulse about 7 times to break the butter into smaller pieces and begin the mixing.

2] In a small bowl or cup, combine the egg yolk and cold water with a fork. With the food processor running, pour the egg mixture through the feed tube and continue processing until the dough holds together and forms a ball around the blade.

3] Tear off two 11-inch lengths of plastic wrap. Place one on a work counter or board and empty the dough onto it. Press the dough to form a disk and then flatten with the palm of your hand. Place the other sheet of plastic on top, so the plastic completely covers the dough, with the disk in the middle. The plastic wrap will prevent sticking and make the dough much easier to work with.

4] Beginning at the center and working outward, making small turns between rolls, lightly roll out the dough to form an 11-inch circle. To line the tart pan, carefully remove the top sheet of plastic. Holding the corners of the bottom sheet, flip the dough over so it covers the bottom and sides of a 10-inch tart pan with removable bottom. Carefully peel off the plastic.

5] Press the dough into the sides and crimp the edges with your index fingers. Run the rolling pin over the top to remove overhanging dough and even out the top. (Extra dough can be used to repair any holes or tears or to build up any thin edges—just press it into place. It also makes excellent cookie dough.) Cover with plastic and reserve in the refrigerator at least 15 minutes or as long as 2 days.

6] To bake an empty tart shell, also called baking blind: Preheat the oven to 425 F. Prick the dough in several places with the tines of a fork and then cover with a sheet of aluminum foil or parchment paper that overhangs by an inch on all sides. Fill the paper with rice, dried beans, or pie weights and bake 10 minutes. Remove the paper with weights (rice and beans may be stored and used again) and bake an additional 10 minutes, until nicely browned.

BOOKS ON FRENCH CUISINE AND CULTURE

Bocuse, Paul. *Paul Bocuse in Your Kitchen*. Pantheon, New York, 1982.
Three-star chef Bocuse wrote this book for beginners after he got his more complicated restaurant recipes off his chest in earlier books. Here he covers all the regional specialties of la cuisine bourgeoise with no extra steps, luxury ingredients, or anecdotes to clutter up the palate or the mind. It is the most reliable, down-to-earth French cookbook on my shelf.

Brillat-Savarin, Jean A. *The Physiology of Taste*. North Point Press, San Francisco, 1986.
Bon vivant, lawyer, and gastronome extraordinaire, Brillat-Savarin spent thirty years researching this idiosyncratic treatise on the pleasures of eating—probably the most quoted food book in the world. (It was published posthumously in 1825.) In case you haven't thought much about the erotic properties of truffles or the influence of gastronomy on business, his is the book to get you started. This edition is lovingly translated by M.F.K. Fisher with plenty of her own asides.

Child, Julia; Louisette Bertholle; Simone Beck. *Mastering the Art of French Cooking*, Volume I. Alfred A. Knopf, New York, 1961.
————. *From Julia Child's Kitchen*. Alfred A. Knopf, New York, 1975.
A lot of time and trends have elapsed since Child first dispensed her wisdom "for the servantless American cook," but Julia remains la Julia—a good-natured culinary monument. If you have the patience and the time to work through all the steps, her books will direct you faultlessly through the entire repertoire of classic French cuisine for the American kitchen, with variations galore.

David, Elizabeth. *French Provincial Cooking*. Michael Joseph, London, 1960.
This renowned English food writer supplied inspiration, recipes, and cookware to a generation of food writers and chefs. Her books, reissued by a British publisher and available at specialty bookstores or by order, are troves of information and feeling for the French way with food. Though the books do have recipes, I find them better for reading than for cooking.

Deighton, Len. *ABC of French Food*. Bantam Books, New York, 1990.
The intrepid writer of suspense novels likes to spend his time eating, cooking, and hanging around with the great chefs of Europe when he is not sitting in front of the word processor. More than a few well-informed opinions have emerged and been set down in this entertaining volume that resembles an author's notebook both in its conversational tone and in the sketches. Good bedtime reading.

Johnston, Mireille. *The Cuisine of the Sun*, Vintage Books, New York, 1976.
————. *The French Family Feast*. Simon & Schuster, New York, 1988.
This Frenchwoman has her subject in her fingertips. Her authentic regional recipes don't omit a detail—the ingredient list for couscous is three pages long—but if you have the time you could do worse than to follow her deft instructions. Definitely not for the beginner, although the Provençal recipes are relatively short and easy.

Olney, Richard. *The French Menu Cookbook*. David R. Godine, Boston, 1985.
————. *Ten Vineyard Lunches*. Interlink Books, New York, 1988.
Olney, an American writer living in Provence, has impeccable taste and a clear writing style that is much admired by fellow writers and chefs. Although I have never cooked his food, one has the feeling that everything this intelligent sensualist touches turns out well.

Root, Waverley. *The Food of France*. Vintage Books, New York, 1992.
Root was an American journalist and foreign correspondent who catalogued whole countries and their relationship to food in his spare time. In this classic he organizes all of France according to preferred cooking fats: butter, lard, or oil. With wonderful descriptions of food, people, and places, it is inspirational reading before a trip to France. Classic regional dishes are described without recipes.

Scotto Sisters. *France: The Beautiful Cookbook*. Collins Publishers, San Francisco, 1989.
This series of big beautiful coffee table books is unusually useful. The recipes are practical, the text informative, and the pictures of both places and food awe-inspiring.

Wells, Patricia. *The Food Lover's Guide to Paris*. Workman, New York, 1984.
————. *The Food Lover's Guide to France*. Workman, New York, 1987.

————. *Bistro Cooking*. Workman, New York, 1989.

———— and Joel Robuchon. *Simply French*. William Morrow, New York, 1991.

Wells is the best contemporary palate working the French food scene today. This relentless researcher, an American journalist living in Paris and Provence, captures the sights, sounds, and smells of artisanal food-makers, restaurants, cafés, and outdoor markets with style, grace, and enthusiasm to burn. The guides are a must for any serious eater traveling in France.

Willan, Anne. *French Regional Cooking*. William Morrow, New York, 1981.

————. *La Varenne Pratique*. Crown, New York, 1989.

Willan, the British/American owner of La Varenne cooking school, is a reliable source if you like your culinary information on the plain and practical side. Her regional book is timeless—a beautifully designed, pho-tographed, and researched tour through the provinces with classic recipes intact; the *Pratique* is an up-to-date reference book with color photographs on classic techniques and ingredients. Both are wonderful gifts for some-one who wants to get serious about cooking.

Wolfert, Paula. *The Cooking of Southwest France*. Dial Press, New York, 1983.

Wolfert, the cookbook writer's cookbook writer, picks a region, lives and breathes it, and then translates it for American cooks. The recipes are precise and sometimes lengthy—the duck confit recipe runs three full text pages—but the results are always full-flavored and first-rate. Southwest France, by the way, is the land of goose fat, foie gras, truffles, and very serious eating.

INDEX

Index

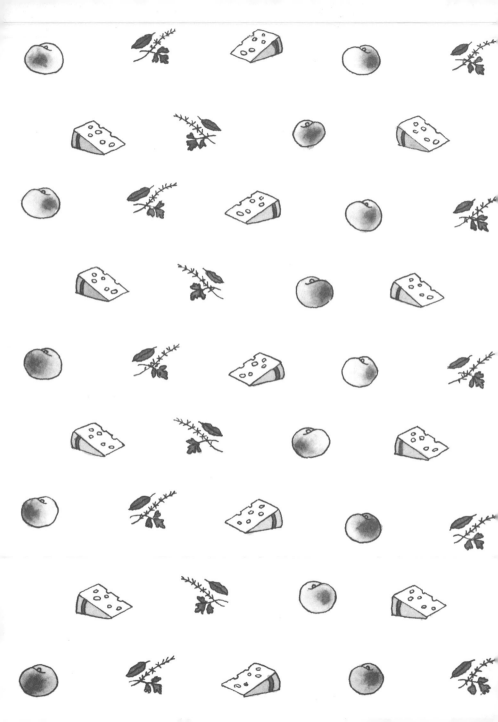